A really helpful guide to product manag[...] help bring the concepts to life. This bo[...] new to product management or some[...] 10+ years. Most importantly, the writin[...] it's an enjoyable read.—**Eric Enders, Product Management Leader**

Product Takeoff is an essential read for anyone looking to bring a new disruptive product to market. The book could have easily been called, *Listen.* Get something out into the world using all the latest thinking that popularizes process and methodology approaches (think Agile, Lean Startup, Design Thinking, etc.) and put it in the hands of customers and then . . . Listen! This approach may not guarantee immediate success, but it darn well will avoid slow, costly failure. Thank you, Kamal and Navjot, for sharing your insights and wisdom with a world hungry to give us the next big thing!—**Richard Sheridan, CEO, Co-founder, and Chief Storyteller, Menlo Innovations, Author of Joy, *Inc.* and Chief Joy Officer**

Product Takeoff demystifies how some companies deliver consistently delightful products. Their framework based on case studies from ubiquitous products and services is an essential reference for anyone who aspires to be a rock star product manager.—**Hugh Molotsi, Innovator, Advisor, and Entrepreneur**

Product Takeoff provides a playbook for teams who want to put their customers first. It's an essential read to build great engaging products!—**SC Moatti, Founding CEO, Products That Count, Managing Partner, Mighty Capital, Bestselling Author, *Mobilized***

Product Takeoff is a compelling read because of its overall product management theme. It opens my mind to new product ideas with the interesting concept and themes. This book is a pleasure to read simply because of its case studies and deep learning it can provide to aspiring product innovators.—**Manik Arora, CEO, Verveba Telecom**

Creating a product that is invaluable to the customer is both an art and a science that requires a blend of innovative thinking and the ability to know what the customer wants (often before they know themselves). The book titled *Product Takeoff* is an invaluable guide, as it covers many ideas and frameworks, along with providing step-by-step instructions for aspiring innovators and product developers to create bleeding-edge products. The road to progress takes many turns, and having a set of frameworks and ideas helps seed innovation, as well as provide tactical steps for execution. *Product Takeoff* is a brilliant guide that serves as a medium for both inspiration and execution, and is a must-read to add to your bookshelf regarding innovative product development.—**Gail Ferreira, PhD, Principal, Boston Consulting Group**

Product Takeoff is a must-read for everyone who cares about building the right products in the right way!—**Amidha Shyamsukha, Product Management Leader**

Product Takeoff

By Kamal Manglani
and Navjot Singh

Happy About

20660 Stevens Creek Blvd., Suite 210
Cupertino, CA 95014

Published by Happy About®
20660 Stevens Creek Blvd., Suite 210, Cupertino, CA 95014
http://happyabout.com

First Printing: September 2018
Hardcover ISBN: 1-60005-279-7 978-1-60005-279-8
Paperback ISBN: 1-60005-278-9 978-1-60005-278-1
eBook ISBN: 1-60005-280-0 978-1-60005-280-4
Place of Publication: Silicon Valley, California, USA
Paperback Library of Congress Number: 2018952987

Trademarks

Warning and Disclaimer

Acknowledgement

This book has been a huge inspiration since the beginning of our friendship and our long discussions over various hurdles faced by executives in the corporate world.

This compilation could not have been completed without the help of many friends, colleagues, and family who have constantly been engaged with discussions and feedback.

For the completion of this work of art, we are highly obliged to:

- Our dear colleagues, for the constant feedback and encouragement.
- Gayatri Sirure and Kristin, for editorial support and suggestions. We appreciate the hard work and commitment they have shown toward their work.
- Our wives, Amita Kaur and Preeti Ahuja, for encouragement, feedback, and pushing us constantly for completion of this book.
- The Happy About team, for their support and management on the timely feedback and constant improvements on the final product.

A special thanks to all our mentors, our product management community, and colleagues whom we have worked with in the past, for the learnings that have been incorporated in us. This would include Devang Mody and Amit Raghuvanshi, for instilling the entrepreneur spirit in me and guiding me toward successful product launches in the past.

Finally, a huge thank you to our students, who have been experimenting with these ideas to build awesome products serving our communities!

C o n t e n t s

Product Takeoff is about making dreams a reality. This book will give you the tools to envision new products and achieve a radical, rapid pace of innovation.

Our concept is partly inspired by the Carousel of Progress[1], a theater show created by Walt Disney for the New York World's Fair in 1964. After the fair, the show ran for years at Disneyland, before finding a permanent home at the Walt Disney World Resort, where it delights visitors to this day.

As the show begins, the audience slowly rotates around a central stage, like a carousel[2]. The first scene opens onto a typical American family at home in their living room in the early 1900s. The family marvels at a dizzying array of new products that have changed their lives—from moving pictures and gas lamps, to an icebox and the telephone. They are certain they have achieved the pinnacle of innovation, and the incredible technology they now enjoy will never be surpassed.

As the carousel turns, we see the same family inside their home in the 1920s. More new inventions surround them: electric light bulbs, indoor plumbing, a radio broadcast delivering the news, and more. They excitedly mention that it's now possible to travel from the East Coast to the West Coast by train in only three days. Once again, they feel technology has reached the highest possible level of imagination—but the carousel continues to turn.

The *Carousel of Progress* was Walt Disney's favorite attraction, and he was deeply involved in its creation[3]. The show looks back on the twentieth-century experience of progress and the incredible advances in the lives of Americans. Surprisingly, the exhibit holds the record for both the longest running stage show and the most performances in American history. Walt Disney intended for the attraction to remain on view forever—as if progress itself should never come to an end.

Even today, in each moment of the *now*, we feel that the cycle of progress is on the verge of take-off, though in the twenty-first century, we've come to understand that each innovation paves the way for the next. With potential beckoning all around us, we recognize both the possibility of failure and an opportunity to increase our learning exponentially.

We are all on the carousel—although at times, it might feel more like a rollercoaster without seatbelts.

Everyone wants to build an awesome product, and every business wants in. But what elements of product management are actually necessary to lift off your growth?

In this book, we'll cover the four major principles of the innovation cycle: *vision, strategy, team, and rapid learning.* We'll demonstrate a systematic method for generating ideas, building a highly collaborative environment, and crafting the customer journey. Our goal is to help you create products that break the Product Life Cycle and enable your company to flourish in a growth stage for a longer period of time.

The core of our process is to start with customer needs and ensure a faster feedback loop; however simple it might sound, this is *the secret recipe for growth in revenue, growth in learning, or both.*

We wish you the best, and we invite you to join us in creating highly scalable and desirable products.

Product Takeoff

1 INNOVATION

Chapter

1 Radical Innovation

"If you can dream it, you can do it."
—Tom Fitzgerald, Disney Imagineer[4]

In one swift move, Apple dropped "computer" from its company name and launched the first-generation iPhone.[5] Steve Jobs had taken a technology that had been around for close to thirty years by that point—the cellular phone—and fused it with a design sensibility and now-famous innovations. At the time, it was seen as a risky, ambitious play. The year was 2007.

The pace hasn't slowed since. One by one, companies in the technology space began to innovate. Netflix launched streaming services in 2007, and Tesla launched the first electric sports car, the Roadster, in 2008. Uber was founded in California in 2009, and yet another innovative juggernaut, Square, launched their financial services in 2010.

Innovation has become a day-to-day topic. At offices, meetup groups, and conventions all across the country, people talk about the latest products and anticipate the next. We speculate about driverless cars changing the world—our children may never have to drive, and accidents on the highway might be a thing of the past.

Not every venture is rewarded, and even the best-known companies make massive mistakes. At the 2015 Consumer Electronic Show (CES) in Las Vegas, many visitors wore Google Glass, a product stopped by Google that same year. Google Glass remains a cautionary tale—when untethered from customer needs, the quest for innovation can backfire spectacularly.

At the same event, Mercedes Benz displayed its powerful and sleek F 015, described by the company as an "innovative perspective into the future of mobility.[6]" The interior of the car was designed to serve as a digital living space that constantly interacts with the passenger, vehicle, and the outside world.

Dr. Dieter Zetsche, chairman of the board of management of Daimler AG and head of Mercedes-Benz Cars said, "The car is growing beyond its role as a mere means of transport and will ultimately become a mobile living space.[7]" When the car takes over from the driver in situations where driving isn't much fun, passengers in self-driving cars will be able to enjoy free time for relaxing or working as they please.

As Zetsche emphasizes in the case of the Mercedes F 015, *there's much more to a product than its technical capabilities.*

With the launch of the iPhone in 2007,
a juggernaut of innovation was unleashed.
Photo by Brandon Ong on Unsplash

Amazon is another leading source of innovation, and the company has been hard at work. Founded in 1994 as an online bookstore, it has come a long way by innovating on many fronts. At Amazon, the MVP (minimum viable product) concept is deployed such that at every stage, products they launch are fully utilized and carry on with the supplemental suite of products that follow. It is not a coincidence that Amazon is one of the most customer-centric companies.

Pricing in retail can be a tricky concept. In the 1990s—back when the only retail option was a brick-and-mortar store—a consumer's biggest disadvantage was not knowing the price of the product at competing stores. For example, to compare prices on Tide detergent, you had to drive to five different stores, and only then would you know which retailer had the cheapest price.

The consumer web has completely revolutionized retail pricing.

Here's a step-by-step example of a consumer planning to buy Tide detergent online:

> 1) Go to Google search.
> 2) Search "Tide."
> 3) Switch to Shopping results for Tide.
> 4) Search for the type of online retailer the consumer wants to use.
> 5) Choose the retailer, go to their website, and purchase.

Google has solved the problem—consumers can now compare prices from twenty-five different retailers for the same product, allowing for fast decision making.

Even when a retailer isn't offering the best price in the comparison, they still need ways to acquire and retain customers. Amazon, once again, delivers a solution.

In 2015, Amazon launched Dash, a Wi-Fi-enabled smart button.[8] In case of detergent, the button can be attached to a washing machine, and it enables one-touch ordering. This might be an innovation for the busy consumer who doesn't have enough time to go online and search for products—or it might be another strategy to wrestle back negotiation power from the same consumer.

With a handy smart button, there's no need to go online and search for Tide. Instead, just push the button, and the product will be delivered the very next day. Since the consumer didn't go online through the purchase cycle, they may not have compared prices (and didn't even think of going to a different store). Is this a win-win strategy for all? It might be if you're the customer who wants to save time, and that's whom Dash is really made for.

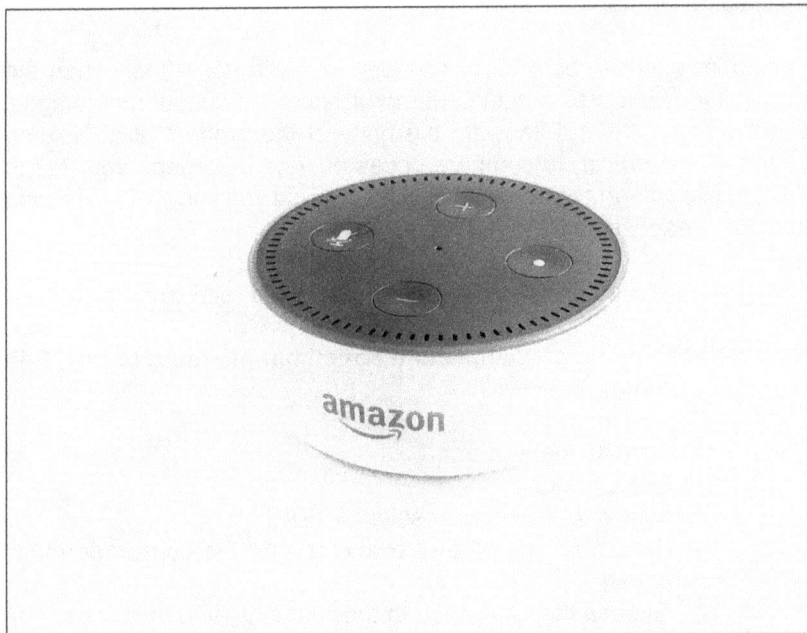

The Amazon Echo delivers a new level of innovation to the consumer web.
Photo by Rahul Chakraborty on Unsplash

In 2016, Amazon launched Echo, a Wi-Fi-enabled multi-use home device. The Echo can play music, podcasts, talk, and listen. It's ready to understand your buying patterns, the movies you watch, and the music you listen to. Re-ordering a favorite product can be done with a simple voice command. The Echo may well be starting another chapter of innovation by taking complete control over our lives. It debuted with basic services like smart lighting, radio, and news but has added more functions—including a cooking and chore virtual assistant.

Year in and year out, innovation in technology is nowhere near stopping—rather, it's moving at a rapid pace and permeating every facet of our world.

But this story is not limited to technology.

Innovation doesn't just occur solely around technology. *Instead, it's about the experiences we create in the most unexpected places.*

At the time of this writing, Magic Castle Hotel was the second-highest-ranked hotel in Los Angeles on TripAdvisor. A basic, comfortable room was nominally priced and otherwise identical to their competitors. However, most reviews mentioned the hotel's unique "Popsicle Hotline" experience. Anyone can request a free popsicle from a dedicated hotline phone near the swimming pool. This simple experience gives customers and their children a lifelong story to remember.

What experiences will you create with innovation?

2 Innovate or Die

A well-known author, speaker, and consultant named George Land published his seminal book, *Grow or Die*, in 1973. At the time, common wisdom held that most companies needed to grow in order to sustain themselves—or else they'd die competing with larger corporations. In the book, Land laid out his theory of transformation and explained how companies can actually thrive in competition. His theory became an important part of planning and strategizing the transformation of organizations.

Jack V. Matson developed these ideas further in his book, *Innovate or Die*. Matson conceives of innovation as an art, and he outlines the various steps and stages of innovation. They include creatively coming up with ideas, sorting out the most promising ideas, testing prototypes, and then launching the idea or product itself. He sets out the philosophy of ITF (Intelligent Test Failure) in which each failure can provide knowledge and help improvise on the idea to finally achieve success.

From "grow or die" to "innovate or die," the underlying philosophy remains much the same. The terms have simply changed to suit the times.

Over the past few years, as organizations have grown larger, they've been forced to slow down—and they've been beaten by smaller start-ups leveraging the new age of technology. Beyond a certain level, even growing larger isn't going to help.

Time and again, big organizations work to create innovative processes. Their size and scale confer certain advantages, and they should be able to create efficiencies in the system. Still, they are often failing to beat new products or processes coming from newer companies that have a strong belief in disruption. For example, large companies like Nokia follow innovation practices and Agile software development but are still struggling to keep pace in the rapidly changing world.[9] How did they go from giants to buyouts snapped up by a larger company's portfolio?

A similar fate lies in wait for Yahoo—once an internet behemoth, but now a company marred by slow growth. Why were they unable to jump over hurdles, even when they saw them coming? Was it about reinventing their platforms or something else altogether?

Both Nokia and Yahoo pursed many "innovative ideas"—*what happened?*

3 Disruption vs. Innovation

In 2012, there were over 233,000 taxi cab drivers in the US,[10] and a person or company needed a taxi medallion (license) to drive a taxi. Today, Uber is the biggest example of digital disruption in the taxicab industry. Through Uber, anybody with a valid license and car can sign up on the platform and become a taxi driver with their own car.

As an innovative platform, Uber disrupts the ride experience and exponentially increases the number of riders and drivers. A few of its core disruptions include: increasing the pool of possibilities for new drivers, accelerating the speed at which they can join and begin work, and many other examples of rider experience.

It is a revolutionary technology to be able to trace the path of your Uber down a busy street or watch it park near your pickup point. Furthermore, with Uber, you have visual confirmation that your car is committed to picking you up. Uber's disruption displaced the existing marketplace of yellow cabs with a more worthwhile experience, and this disruption would not be possible without the technological innovation of the Uber app.

No need to scan the streets for these old-school signs,
it's all on your smartphone.
Photo by Peter Kasprzyk on Unsplash

Uber is an example of PAAS (Platform As A Service) in that it allows both drivers and riders to be consumers of services on the platform. PAAS is growing at a rapid pace, and most industries are moving resources into these technologies.

A few years ago, PayPal introduced a money transfer system through which people could transfer money using email ID instead of bank accounts. This triggered a cascade of transformation in the banking and payment-processing industries.

Email ID will become the most powerful tool for individuals and contain more details about a person's history than their social security number. Today, parents have started registering email IDs for newborn babies or even as soon as they decide on a name. They will be assigned to children right in their hospital bed, much like a dealership issuing a number plate for a car as soon as it's ready to go out on the road.

Imagine using an email ID for assigning a bank account, getting utilities, and signing up on social media accounts. It will have a detailed history of any person's past and present—and in certain cases, predict their future behavior patterns.

Chapter 3: Disruption vs. Innovation

The wireless industry has further enabled the spread of PAAS. The speed of data over devices like mobile phones has become as fast as high-speed internet, which was formerly available only to corporate users or at a very high price. The price of data transfer has gone down considerably, ensuring availability of high-speed internet to almost every user in the US.

The possibilities opened up by digital disruption have just begun to manifest. Lending Club makes it possible for anyone to become a lender. Through peer-to-peer lending, people get returns on the money lying idle in their bank accounts and can diversify their portfolio beyond traditional stock market or gold investments. Individuals can be their own bank and lend as much money as they're able, with good returns on their portfolio. This might be the end of the banking industry—or a time to re-innovate. Imagine a world where we don't have to go to a bank to get a loan, because twenty individuals on a Lending Club platform can fund any needs we have.

PAAS has surpassed the imaginary line of innovation in almost all industries, including hospitality, banking, travel, retail, and so on. As new platforms emerge, the experience for both consumers and service providers increases exponentially.

PAAS enables users to connect on unprecedented scale.
Which industry is next?

Uber has been successful in most countries, even if there is a huge disjoint in the way different countries embrace technology. The technology is widely available, but it's a country's *willingness* that makes adoption of an innovation possible.

Despite the fact that we live in a globalized world, disruption isn't taking place at the same pace across all continents. There are various reasons for that gap, and positive reasons why the timeline of implementation has at least been reduced. But major launches still do not occur in real time. Most of the world economies aren't innovating simultaneously, but instead follow a kind of "waiting period" to receive new technology rollouts. If Mercedes today can launch a new car at the same time across the globe in different countries, why can't companies like Airbnb or Lending Club do the same?

We're not there yet—different cultures and government policies are still not on the same platform and are prone to clash at intersections.

The technology disruption is slowly but surely dissolving that divide, but it will take time. When disruption arrives, we'll know it—it will uproot our patterns of thought, behavior, and even the way we do business day-to-day. We'll continue to see a trend where entire industries are disrupted by innovations in technology like block chain, AI, autonomous vehicles, and much more to come.

4 Listen First, Innovation Follows

Mindset is the decisive factor in our ability to effectively disrupt within a rapidly changing marketplace. Success hinges on the way we think and adapt to the environment—and more than ever before, the environment itself is a complex web of customer needs. To make innovative products, *we must be as close to the customer as possible.*

Feel free to ignore this message . . . at your own peril. Years of research and development on Google Glass might have led to a successful product—instead of a flop—if the engineering team had paid careful attention to real customer needs and desires. Instead, customer reactions became apparent *after* the launch.

One way or another, you'll be hearing from your customer—why not start as early as possible?

Only through proximity to the customer will we discover the right problem to solve. Go out into the field. Watch people interacting in the real-world environment where the product will be used. Passively observe, take notes, and actively interview people to understand what they're doing, what they like, and what they dislike. Hearing the voice of the customer helps reframe what we thought the problem was and what it actually is.

To innovate, a company needs to carefully frame a customer's problem via these two steps:
1) Succinctly understand the customer's story.
2) Accurately reach the depth of the problem.

For each product or service, there is both an abstract concept of that product or service that exists in our minds and on the other, the real-time experience we have when using it.

As we've seen from the example of Google Glass, we should empathize until we fully understand the customer's personal experience and how they feel about the product.

Customer empathy is a crucial precondition for generating insights. If Google engineers had empathized with their customers, they would have realized the product caused social awkwardness, among other problems.

To empathize with the customer, we need to spend significant amounts of time with them—talking and listening—until we really get under the hood and understand their needs. Insights arise out of these sessions of non-judgmental observation and listening.

For example, why do people use pencils to tie hair? If you look at the problem strictly from the outside, it might seem random or superficial. On the other hand, you could engage your curiosity and empathy to uncover the hidden logic.

If you talk to folks who use pencils as hair ties, you might discover hidden needs. For example, they keep losing hair ties, which they find to be a problem; they like the shape the pencil gives to their up-do; they prefer the sensation to a constricting hair tie; or their only alternative, a rubber band, sticks to their hair and inevitably pulls out strands. With just a single question, you can uncover networks of customer needs.

Empathy maps are a popular tool for mapping insights about customers. We won't discuss empathy maps in depth, but here's an exercise to build up your skills: try to build an empathy map for a person using a toothbrush. Join your significant other or housemate in the bathroom for minute or two, and quietly observe their simple routine—it's probably different than yours. What insights do you develop based on watching someone brush their teeth?

What do you see? There are a thousand possibilities . . .
Photo by Yoann Siloine on Unsplash

Careful listening is the key to product management. Yet, within the over-all skill of listening, there are many sub-skills to practice and master. The more you're able to empathize with and understand your customers, the more you'll be primed to deliver creative business insights.

Listening techniques to increase your customer empathy:
1) Use positive body language.
2) Hold mock interviews with your audience.
3) Actively visualize what the speaker is saying.

What do they feel?

What do they hear?

What do they think?

What do they see?

PAIN
What are their fears?
Obstacles & frustrations?

GAIN
What do they want or need?
How do they measure success?

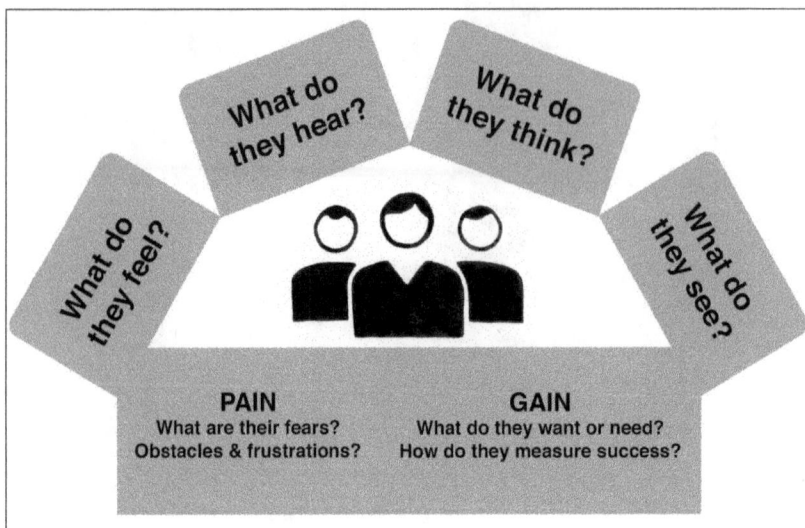

4) Give feedback.
5) Ask clarifying questions.
6) Be silent and don't offer suggestions.

1) Use positive body language
These days, diverted attention is a huge problem. It is particularly difficult to capture attention when your conversation partner is doing other things. There are distractions all around us, like surfing the internet or repeated phone checking. Positive body language demonstrates your interest, engages your conversation partner, and warmly encourages them to continue. It's not hard to show a positive listening response—simply nod, lean forward, and otherwise visibly show interest in the topic. Doing so will make a big difference in your ability to connect and empathize.

2) Hold mock interviews with your audience
This is an important tool for developing an understanding of your customers. Interviews can have huge impact on the way the overall business discussion needs to be framed or re-directed. When you start a conversation with an open-ended question, you're often more likely to receive insights that can help you understand the customer's likes, dislikes, and how they feel and perform under different situations. Mock interviews may also involve role-playing exercises, which can set up test scenarios and help you understand what drives the customer into a particular direction.

Chapter 4: Listen First, Innovation Follows

3) Actively visualize what the speaker is saying

We're all familiar with the phrase, "Pictures speak louder than words." In this case, when you try to create a picture of what your conversation partner is trying to say, it will be easier for your brain to focus—especially if the topic is complex or time consuming. The process of forming the image will be a kind of visual mapping, as a potential source of creative insight in itself. If your thoughts move away from the topic, try to refocus by returning to the image.

4) Give feedback

Consistent feedback will minimize confusion that arises during the discussion—and some degree of confusion or lack of clarity is nearly guaranteed. Feedback also ensures that both parties are still interested and want to keep moving forward. If you notice any confusion or if things seem unclear, always try to paraphrase your participant's questions, opinions, and perspectives.

5) Ask clarifying questions

Usually, a confusing topic will move your attention away from listening. You'll end up tuning out the new information, and it won't help you discover what you want to know. Clarifying questions keep you engaged in the learning process. They also help signal to your conversation partner what stage of learning you're at, which enables them to tailor the message you match your needs. Asking clarifying questions helps you maintain a constant interest in the topic and helps your conversation partner determine the best way to deliver information.

6) Be silent and don't offer suggestions

Offering suggestions detracts from the glory of your audience. They have information or stories they'd like to tell you. It's their time to shine—but interruptions upset the delicate balance and make you the center of attention. Always remain silent, and don't put words in the other person's mouth. Similarly, your questions should be formulated with care. Avoid asking leading questions or those that have a yes/no answer.

Imagine that our company has recently launched several cookies, and we'd like to figure out which flavor is best. To get an answer, we carefully perform a standardized exercise with our customers, and during the feedback process, we ask them, "Do you think the strawberry flavor is better than the chocolate?" Unfortunately, this question is both suggestive and close-ended—and it's unlikely to get us the valuable feedback we're looking for. Instead, the entire feedback process should be formulated so the customer is able to say, "Strawberry is a common flavor for cookies, why not have a raspberry flavor?"

Conscious listening creates an understanding of what your customer *actually needs*. By employing conscious listening and the specific techniques we've outlined, you'll be able to effectively engage customers and help them feel comfortable, affirmed, understood, and able to speak openly. Having set the stage, you will be able to gather the valuable information and insights you need.

We believe listening and interviewing skills should be modeled on those of Oprah. Across her many shows and platforms, she has one common denominator: *she always listens to and validates her guests.*

When we speak, whether we are aware of it or not, fundamental unconscious desires are at work. Oprah meets our inmost need to be listened to, and as a result, she's able to bring out the best in her guests.

During a conversation between Oprah and spiritual leader Thích Nhất Hạnh,[11] Nhất Hạnh spoke about the healing power of deep and compassionate listening. He described the state of listening beautifully, saying, "You listen with only one purpose: to help him or her to empty his heart. Even if he says things that are full of wrong perceptions, full of bitterness, you're still capable of continuing to listen with compassion."[12]

Nhất Hạnh also explicitly cautions against any kind of interruption, especially the hubris of advice. He continues, "If you want to help him to correct his perception, you wait for another time. For now, you don't interrupt. You don't argue."

The act of deep listening has a greater purpose, which Nhất Hạnh describes as an ability to bring about profound change. As he said, "One hour like that can bring transformation and healing."

After we generate insights into customer needs—with the confidence that comes from effective customer research—we can come up with ideas. More and more ideas can be generated and combined to reach a point where we begin to filter and eventually arrive at the best idea that can be implemented. Once an optimal idea is decided on, we begin the phase of experimenting and learning, which can then be built into the concrete experience, and a real product is ready to be brought to life.

Every situation has a unique nexus of customer problems and values, rock stars included.

Photo by Oscar Keys on Unsplash

In early days of rock 'n' roll, the only way singers could hear their performance was by placing speakers pointed directly at them on the stage as they performed. Considering the decibel level, there was a lot of feedback from their performance.

Due to the effects of loud music over time, a large number of rock stars have lost their hearing, including legends like Eric Clapton, Phil Collins, and Ozzy Osbourne.

Shure, a company known for designing and selling microphones, once faced a huge problem. Microphone sales were dropping due to singers suffering from hearing loss. The only way they could get their sales back up was to design something that would help eradicate the phenomenon. Shure came up with an idea to replace the wedges, or onstage speakers, with earbuds. Sales did not go up, and singers even refused to use earbuds—they projected the wrong image. Earbuds were typically used by older people with hearing problems, a reputation that didn't mesh with their rock-star lifestyle. The product solved a requirement, but at the same time, it created an impediment for the customer.

Shure went back and spent time with their customers—the rock 'n' roll singers. And this time, they listened.

The team began to empathize with the customer emotionally, as well as develop a detailed understanding their professional demands. After a few in-depth customer research sessions and ongoing Q&A, it became obvious that earbuds wouldn't make the singers feel comfortable. Earbuds disrupted their "cool" image, which affected their ability to connect with the audience.

This exercise allowed them to design a new strategy. By clearly realizing what didn't work, they were able to come up with a product that singers could use without destroying their public persona, while preserving their hearing. They called this new product, the "personal stage monitor."

Personal stage monitors have earpieces that are isolated from the microphone, thus reducing the potential for feedback loops. They help singers block out noise, while giving them the power to control and monitor the stage volume.

Shure rebranded the entire concept of personal stage monitors. It was a bold move but also one that was carefully derived from customer research and an understanding of the full scope of the customer problem. The product became exciting for singers and increased sales volumes for Shure while solving an integral medical problem.

2 HOW TO BE A VISIONARY PRODUCT MANAGER LIKE ELON MUSK

Chapter

5 | How to Be a Visionary Product Manager Like Elon Musk

"The only way to win is to learn faster than anyone else."

— *Eric Ries,* The Lean Startup

A simple, solitary tweet prompted Tesla to release a new feature in just six days.

On December 10, 2016, a Twitter user wrote, "@ elonmusk the San Mateo supercharger is always full with idiots who leave their tesla for hours even if already charged."[13]

Musk responded from his account within hours, "You're right. This is becoming an issue. Supercharger spots are meant for charging. not parking. Will take action."

Just six days later,[14] Tesla announced a new policy at supercharger stations across the US designed to correct the issue—effective immediately—along with supporting updates to the Tesla app.

For publicly traded corporations, a single tweet about a product issue is unlikely to receive a response, *let alone from the CEO.* And it certainly wouldn't be addressed with product updates *within one week.*

Innovative leaders like Elon Musk are setting a new bar for Product Management—even if they don't include Product Manager in their job title.

A wide-open charging station, thanks to a single tweet.
Photo by Chase Lewis on Unsplash

Customers don't want to know about features, stories, or releases. *They just want to know how you're going to help them.*

What value are you bringing to your customer? This isn't necessarily what you think is cool! Only when you demonstrate that you accurately understand your customer's needs and have the tools to solve them will a customer perceive you as a strategic partner.

Product Management is very loosely defined—so much so, that two departments within the same company can use the function of Product Management in different ways. Product Management isn't always the same as Product Development. Furthermore, there's no documented standard of Product Management that is true across companies—so Product Management is, and can be, very specific to a particular firm.

We can think of Product Management as *a company's commitment to managing the lifecycle of the products and customer needs.* A Product Manager is a mini business owner, a general manager, and often thought of as CEO (or mini CEO) of the product. The Product Manager is responsible for leading a cross-functional product development team. This doesn't mean the team has to report to the Product Manager—instead, the team optimizes the product based on the customer and market needs.

Product Managers are very entrepreneurial. They get people to see the endgame and hook them into this vision. Sometimes, Product Managers demonstrate key skills to help their team navigate the politics in a given situation. They know their customer best. They know their market the best. They're the team's expert when it comes to the customer and the market.

The buzz around Product Management keeps growing. The topic continues to gain popularity in the industry, and entire schools of thought around it have been created. We often meet skeptics, who think the role is really for a glorified business analyst, handing off smaller requirements to an agile team on a regular cadence. And we meet non-skeptics, who think the role is essential to bring value in delivery and focus to software development efforts.

Many companies define the means to manage their business results via products. This function is known as Product Management, a combination of discipline, function, and department. For these companies,

Product Management has end-to-end accountability for the products and services that the customers or stakeholders utilize—for example, Facebook, Gmail, Spotify, Kindle, etc.

In the context of software development, a customer is the entity who pays for a service/product, such as the website, mobile app, etc. used by the customer. Some products don't have a direct service fee but monetize the number of customers as a financial outcome. For example, Gmail is free for public users; however, every user sees advertisements, which become a source of revenue for Gmail.

But these Product Management disciplines are not far from traditional business analyst functions, which have existed in our industry for a very long time. True Product Management is a core driver for sustainable growth and innovation in a team or enterprise. Innovation isn't one person's job, and it doesn't happen by creating or managing a backlog of prioritized features.

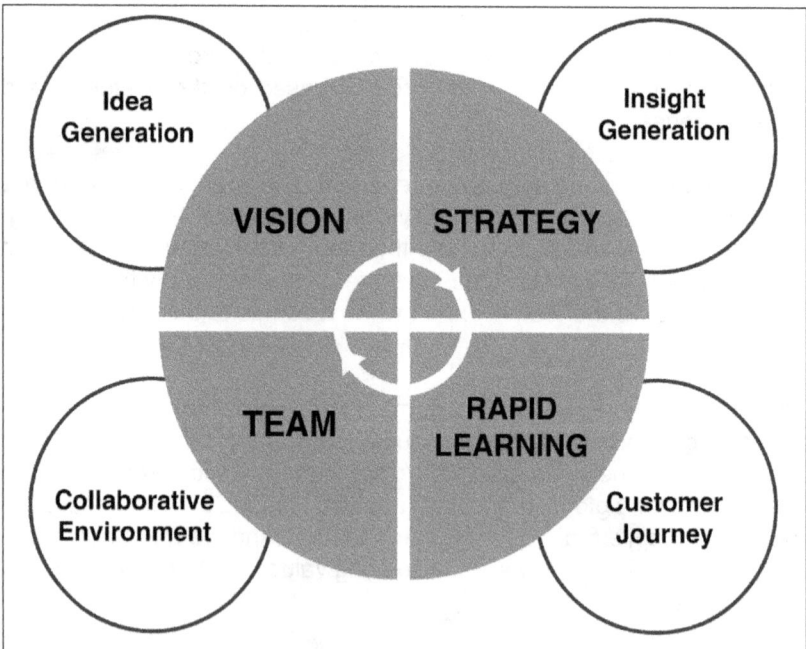

The Innovation Cycle: Vision, Strategy, Rapid Learning, and Team

Chapter 5: How to Be a Visionary Product Manager Like Elon Musk

Let's zoom out of the politics for a moment and take a look at the bird's-eye view of Product Management as a department and function.

As we explore what's under the hood of great Product Management, these four elements emerge:
1) **Vision:** A clear need identified for the customers
2) **Strategy:** A simple but powerful solution
3) **Rapid learning:** Fast experimentation
4) **Team:** A group that perseveres every day to get closer to the vision

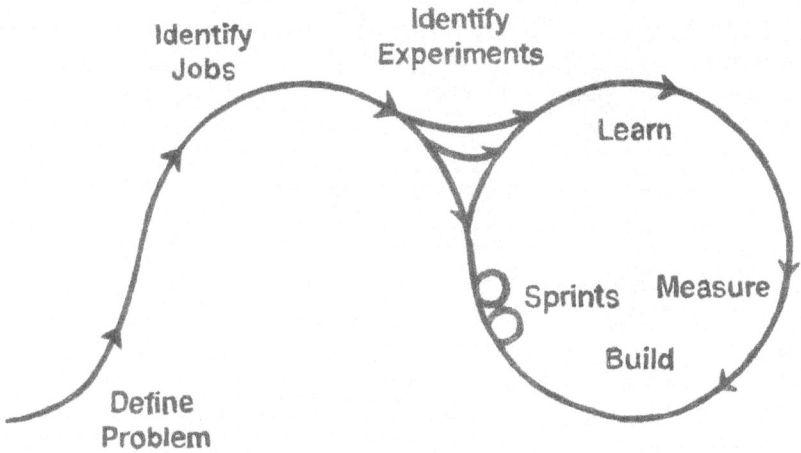

Understanding Product Management from a big picture view means taking a step back.

This book isn't just about practices that support Product Management but also about understanding the building blocks of real breakthroughs.

Product Management decides on a direction by using various techniques. These can be broken down as: *Design Thinking, Lean Startup,* and *Agile.* With Design Thinking, the problem statement is identified by studying the behavior of customers in their native environment. This helps Product Management identify experiments or hypotheses to be tested.

Lean Startup techniques help create multiple iterations of tests using a build-measure-learn loop. The objective is to learn quickly, so Product Management can identify the core set of metrics to be evaluated, e.g., user adoption rates month-on-month, return visits rates per day for Facebook, etc.

Many companies such as Amazon go further by defining a press release for the product they're working on even before writing the first line of code. They also predict the type of customer reviews their products will get on their site, Twitter, or other forums. This measure helps define the instrumentation or forums they want to use to learn more.

Build is based on using Agile software development principles to take the entire product through quick customer feedback loops. This involves writing tests up front, incremental releases and continuous delivery, and a craftsman-like attention to writing good quality code.

There are more than a few common pitfalls. Many Product Managers assume they know what the problem is at the outset and start to write requirements or user stories for developers without further inquiry. This approach is very flawed and is the most common issue encountered in non-customer-oriented product development.

Out of confusion, many companies only apply Agile to building software, but Product Management helps create the overall culture of innovation.

The big picture for Product Management is based on these principles of Design Thinking, Lean Startup, and Agile. The loops are iterative, and all three must be used together in a holistic manner. They also don't follow a logical order. Our learning redirects us to the parts that are most important. The key is to understand the cycle time across the entire loop, which can be minimal, sometimes lasting even less than a day.

At the core, Product Management is about fast learning using the above principles. Some Product Managers are great partakers in the loop; others are awesome at facilitating a team's progress at traversing the loop. The essence of the job is gauging how quickly the team can learn. This is the single most important responsibility of the Product Manager role.

Much like startups, many large companies have started a "pivot ceremony" on a biweekly basis—it's a method to stop the burn of precious development capacity on ideas that aren't working.

Some pivots may take time to realize. Pivots help us realize our promise to get to the vision of solving a customer problem or need, but in an experimental way. Inevitably, there should be fluidity in any strategy to obtain a vision, especially during the early stages of product development.

When the path ahead is dark, fast learning and rapid iterations will reduce the cost of uncertainty.

If there is one change we would like to see in the Product Management function of large companies today, it's that they should re-invent themselves as the *learning champions of their customer needs*.

For innovation to take place, Product Management needs to be considered a learning function within a company. Backlogs are not commitments that need to be met by a given date—they're a mere hypothesis about what we want to learn. Market pressures apply to already existing product increments and must be followed with a great deal of caution without violating the above principles.

What if we have a large platform to overhaul—how do we accomplish it in short iterations? It must be fixed and there's no way out. So, how are we going to learn quickly? Why do we need to use the lean startup principles of *Build-Measure-Learn* to get partial parts of the platform quickly?

This is a great set of questions coming up in large enterprises, especially those that have severe *tech debt*, or even *innovation debt*. Sometimes the reverse is also true, in that we over-innovate but don't really take the product to the customer quickly enough. We'll talk more about this in the next chapter.

3 DIFFERENTIATING PM SKILLS— RAPID LEARNING

Part 3: DIFFERENTIATING PM SKILLS—RAPID LEARNING

6 Rapid Learning for Large Platforms

"Want to increase innovation?
Lower the cost of Failure."

— Joichi Ito, MIT Media Labs[15]

Technical Product Management as a field is evolving toward highly platform-oriented solutions. Let's start by talking about what a platform is.

We have examples of platforms all around us: Uber, LinkedIn, Lyft, and so on. Each platform enables users to provide and sell their services, and the owner of the platform may earn a commission.

The producer and consumer of the service varies depending on the type of platform. For example, both Lyft and Uber provide a platform for car owners to offer driving services in order to help riders. Drivers use the Uber or Lyft app as a platform to find fares, while riders use the app as a platform to search for a ride. The service offered by the drivers is a product, based on the type of ride the user selects, such as POOL, uberX, Lyft Lux, and so on.

We are moving away from independent product offerings and into crowdsourcing product ideas via platforms. Think of platforms as a business model for creating and exchanging value. Successful platforms identify both creators and consumers as primary customer personas and design around this premise at minimum cost.

Facebook is another ubiquitous platform. Though you might not think of them as such (and yourself, if you have an account), its over 2.2 billion monthly users[16] are content creators. The service is free of charge and advertisements are one source of revenue. But the product is the subscriber—yes, every Facebook user is a product, and a unique product at that. You'll notice that in this example, the definition of a product changes from a technology to a subscription.

The monetization of platforms varies. LinkedIn is another example. Members sometimes pay premium services for job applications. In this model, the creators of the profiles on LinkedIn are products, and the creators of job descriptions are also products, attracting consumers to LinkedIn.

In early 2017, LinkedIn changed the entire look and feel of its app, seemingly in one go.[17] It's reasonable to imagine that it was a long project, requiring the development effort of many teams. How would a Product Manager in such a scenario release it iteratively?

At its core, Platform Product Management is about designing an exchange layer to conduct transactions between various layers of the stack. Being technical may be more helpful in some cases. You might not be an active developer writing code, but having enough technical knowledge to understand the details will make your support more effective. For example, a sign-on page may need to interact with sign-on application services using the sign-on API. The sign-on API will be part of the decoupling API developed between the two layers.

Let's say we have a mobile app that also wants to authenticate a user. It would use the same sign-on API as the webpage. Platform Product Management is about solving the problem irrespective of the access channel, whether it's web, mobile, MWEB, other code, etc.

The crux of the idea is about making it easy for developers to build decoupled services on the platform. For example, a click-on-user-profile calls the set of services to render the profile information in a certain way. Can these services be decoupled enough to be built separately and launched iteratively, rather than a "big bang" launch?

It's the Product Manager's decision to launch all in one go or to launch for a limited set of users. A partial launch might use vehicles like A/B testing, where a small percentage of users will get the new experience and a set of metrics will be monitored continuously to provide feedback for the next set of decisions on what to build.

Some startups have taken this to a new level by not engaging in a single line of new code development and instead, heading over to YouTube. The Dropbox founding team tried this route rather famously. During the lengthy product development phase, Dropbox CEO Drew Houston narrated a simple demo video illustrating basic features of the service.[18] A surprising level of interest in the video—and the substantial click-through rate of interested users—gave the team confidence to build a minimal set of viable features for Dropbox.

Platform development efforts may vary. Many companies have successfully monetized platform development, Apple being a case in point. They charge a fee for their developer platform.[19]

Facebook's developer platform is similar. Developers use tools available from Facebook for social sign-on or build feeds to and from the portal. The role of platform Product Manager is defined by the primary consumer of their product, which in most companies, is another technology role: a developer. The platform allows Facebook's mobile app store offerings to grow, keeps end-customers engaged, and helps retain customers.

Product Management on such product platforms will be a mix of fairly technical folks and people who can relate to the development community of startups, companies, and independent developers.

Sometimes the best and most effective platform products are developed outside a large enterprise. SAP recruited a number of university students and installed them in a converted East German railway building outside of Berlin—a safe space conducive to creativity.[20] As a result, the student team built Hasso's New Architecture, now called HANA, which allows data to be stored in a server's main memory, instead of using relational databases.[21] The discovery, and products that followed, allowed SAP to establish a footing both in the database business and cloud computing.

One of SAPS's co-founders, Hasso Plattner, convinced T-Mobile to try a HANA-based product by offering a guarantee: SAP wouldn't charge if it didn't provide results. T-Mobile soon saw the immense market potential of the product. At the time, T-Mobile was looking to lure customers into signing up for new data plans, and to do this, they offered millions of customers variations on data plan offers. T-Mobile needed to be able to study how customers responded to these offers and promote ones that received a positive response. But conventional data warehouse systems took days to return this information. After installing HANA, the wait time was reduced to a few minutes. This was a huge breakthrough, and T-Mobile was able to promote better offers to its customers.

Safecast.org is another excellent example of lean platform product development.[22]

After Japan's devastating earthquake and tsunami, and the subsequent meltdown of the Fukushima Daiichi Nuclear power plant in 2011, accurate and trustworthy information on radiation levels was difficult to obtain and largely unavailable. Safecast was formed in response. Through a mostly volunteer effort, the work of monitoring, collecting, and openly sharing information on environmental radiation was begun.

Today, Safecast provides more radiation data than any large government or privately sponsored project. The simple idea of assembling a Geiger counter to measure radiation levels such that they can be easily carried or attached to cars has enabled a vast network of volunteers to provide the world's largest source of data on radiation levels. The platform built by Safecast enables volunteers to quickly measure, monitor, and upload readings. The device assembly and upload process is taught at local meetups by volunteers, to volunteers, and has become one of the largest platform development efforts ever. Most volunteers form an informal community to teach each other and further grow the community.

In each of the above examples—from Dropbox CEO Drew Houston launching a simple video to test features, to the creative incubation of HANA by SAP co-founder Hasso Plattner—do you see an essence of good Product Management?

If you're a Product Manager working toward platform development, there's a four-part roadmap that will enable you to scale the development effort and adoption.

Once again, the four elements of great Product Management are: *vision, strategy, rapid learning, and teamwork.*

> **Vision:** A clear need identified for the customers
> **Strategy:** A simple but powerful strategy
> **Rapid learning:** Fast experimentation
> **Team:** A group that perseveres every day to get closer to the vision

Find the consumers of your platform product, and co-create the platform with them through simple and early releases, enabling you to learn quickly. Don't assume you know the problem. Instead, *iterate and iterate again* as you continue to learn more about the optimal problem to solve.

7 Customer Journey Map

"You've gotta start from the Customer Experience and work back toward the technology, not the other way around."

— Steve Jobs[23]

When starting product development, the most powerful place to begin is with the basics. However simple they might sound, the fundamentals can't be skipped.

Carefully attending to these three fundamental points will make a vast difference in your outcome:

- How much do we know about the customer and integration points?
- How can that information be verified?
- What are the challenges in the integration points?

Let's consider a parking situation that people encounter daily. Each workday, Susan has a two-hour commute from the East Bay to San Francisco. The train station has limited parking options, and reserve parking availability has a years-long waitlist. Susan drives her car from home to the parking lot, which takes twenty minutes. On some days, she drops her child off at school, which takes an additional ten minutes. The walk from the parking lot to BART adds ten minutes, and her wait for the train adds another ten minutes. The train ride is forty-five minutes. Finally, the walk from the San Francisco train station to her office takes twenty minutes.

So, on an ideal day, Susan has a one-way travel time of 115 minutes, which puts her at almost four hours of travel per day. Assuming she gets a good pay and is very satisfied with her job, how could she save time during her commute? What options does she have for leading a healthier life?

Before we begin the solution process, let's dig deeper into the problem. We're not looking to reinvent the wheel (or design the next Hyperloop). Instead, let's look for small steps that can provide 80 percent improvement.

To do this, we need to take a closer look at Susan's needs, which might be spending more time having fun with her kids or helping with their homework.

There are many solutions to Susan's commute problem:
1) Carpooling
2) Bike to train station and to work from station
3) Work from home a few days per week
4) Change job
5) Improve train frequency
6) Improve train speed
7) Rent an apartment in the city closer to work
And so on . . .

Some of these solutions could be combined. Also, the value of the solution could be entirely dependent on the user—perhaps Susan's preferred options are #1 and #3. The customer journey map reveals different solutions that might vary in value for different types of customers. This is its power.

In December 2016, Elon Musk tweeted, "Traffic is driving me nuts. Am going to build a tunnel boring machine and just start digging . . ."[24] Instead of the options laid out above, Musk would prefer to drill a hole to get to work faster.

This tool helps us build empathy with a particular type of target customer. Imagine the plethora of carpool mobile applications that could be targeted to customers who would enjoy carpooling.

Customer journey maps also help us become proactive about the problem we're trying to solve. *Many Product Managers do things because their manager or analytics expert says so.* However, those actions may be too late. If you don't want to be left behind, the customer journey map is a powerful approach for developing insight.

Let's look at another customer journey map from the ecommerce world: how does a potential customer search, select, and check out a product they want to purchase?

In this case, let's assume the customer is a thirty-eight-year-old mother of a nine-year-old child. Mom wants to find an ideal birthday gift for her daughter, whose birthday is coming up in three weeks. Her daughter likes to color and craft. So, Mom decides to buy her a special art box full of color pencils, sketch pens, crayons, and watercolors.

Most moms today begin their search on a tablet device, such as an iPad. They go to Google and search keywords. Based on the results, they might arrive at links for products on Amazon or other ecommerce sites. Alternatively, a mom might go to a neighborhood store, such as Walgreens or Target, and make a purchase. In this case, let's assume our customer is an ecommerce-savvy buyer.

A global network of commerce is mediated by a simple touch of the screen.
Photo by Timothy Muza on Unsplash

After arriving at a retail website, Mom browses the search results. Depending on the retailer, this may be a simple or a painful experience. Most customers choose not to continue browsing after landing on search results. Retailers might have 95 percent of their traffic landing on irrelevant pages, causing them to bounce off to another site, hoping for better results. This would rarely happen in a walk-to-the-store experience because the investment from the customer to get into a physical store is higher.

Let's say Mom liked the second item in the search rankings and decided to click on it to find out more. Most retailers call this *search relevance metrics*. Amazon's customer focus helps their team keep search so highly tuned that customers usually see what they're looking for in the first few search items returned.

Knowing your customer journey map inside and out helps you focus on the right customer problems. If you see that customers are skipping from the search results page to another site, don't be discouraged—*it signifies an opportunity.*

Amazon implemented "buy with one click" to shorten their customer buying funnel. They realized that with each click, the likelihood of losing their customer grew significantly. Rather than have the customer go through the entire funnel, the team worked out an option to buy with one click. This one feature helped increase the number of checkouts significantly.

1) Starbucks

A customer journey map for Starbucks shows you how the guests inside a Starbucks interact with the service the barista offers.

Starbucks launched its mobile app ordering and payment system in 2015, but the lines at many Starbucks stores have increased. After using the app, customers assume their orders will be ready when they arrive, but are in for a surprise when they have to compete with walk-in customers for the barista's service.

The customer experience map clearly shows that only one barista is available, not two separate baristas catering for either mobile orders or walk-in orders.

2) Target

Plotting a customer journey map for Target self-checkout customers shows that lines in the self-checkout lane are far greater than counters where a cashier takes the payment. This insight can help direct the company to employ a simpler UI, so the self-checkout experience can proceed quickly.

3) Buying a car

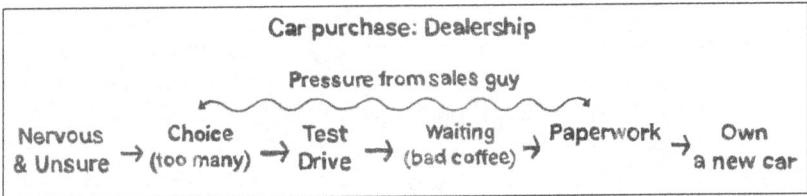

This example demonstrates how our customer is feeling at different points in the process of buying a car. As we see, there are many lows and highs—if we're savvy, that indicates a tremendous amount of opportunity.

Sales folk who are aware of this make every effort to keep your experience on the higher side, thus securing your sale and leaving you with enough positive experience to come back for a second car.

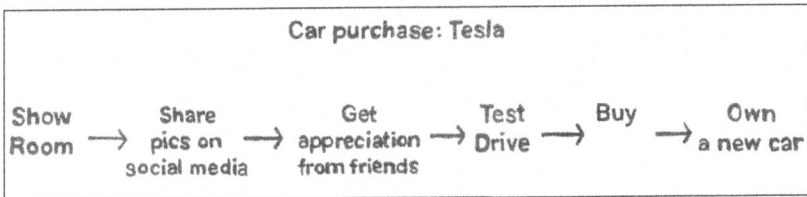

Similarly, building a customer journey map for your competition will reveal a great deal of insight about how they treat their customers. Car dealerships could learn a lot from the Tesla customer journey.

4) Apple Store

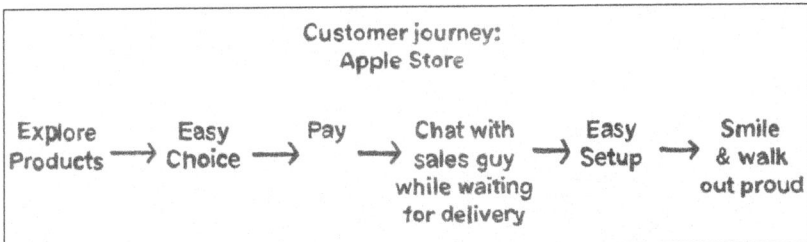

A customer journey map determines why some purchases become memories, while others make you feel as if you paid too much.

Apple stores follow an ultimate customer experience journey: when you make a purchase, the sales agent doesn't let you leave the store with negative thoughts. They talk with you, asking what grade your child is in, and what you plan to use the device for. All of this happens while another Apple employee collects your new device, then hands it over to your salesperson.

Compare this with the experience of buying an expensive device at another store, where the salesperson heads to the back room, leaving you alone to think about the expense you just incurred.

The process of identifying and mapping your customer journey will inevitably reveal areas of potential innovation.

What is your customer journey map?

8 Data-Based Decision Making

> *"Errors using inadequate data are much less than those using no data at all."*
>
> — Charles Babbage[25]

Decision making happens at every step in an organization and at every step in our daily lives. Some decisions are easy to make, others are tough. Usually, difficult and important decisions are made by the most senior or experienced people in an organization or household. The difference is scale: in a household, the scale is small, and a poor decision can more easily be controlled or reversed. But in big organizations, with thousands of employees and millions to billions of dollars at stake, wrong decisions can wreak a massive havoc.

In earlier times, decision making was a less structured process. Most organizations made decisions based on intuitions and emotions, so the chance of failure in a given instance was much higher. On the other hand, this also drove their ability to take risk. Good and well-known leaders made bad decisions, leading to huge losses and in some cases, even bankruptcy or closure of the business.

Over the years, organizations have grown in every possible dimension—number of employees, customers, transactions, revenue, and so on—which has helped them collect enormous amounts of data about every aspect of their business. This data has helped companies understand their businesses better than ever before. They're more aware of the many aspects of their business, and the information is being used intelligently.

Software and statistical algorithms help businesses process a deluge of data. The intelligent outcomes they return assist management in determining when to launch a product and what the outcome of the launch will be.

Across industries, what are the basic questions a Product Manager needs to answer in order to access data? What methods should be used to reliably acquire data and drive solutions? Below, we provide a range of methods.

MARKET RESEARCH

When an organization needs to gather new opinions or better understand an aspect of the business, market research is employed as a primary strategy. For example, if a clothing company wants to launch a new line of clothes, market research will help determine what the customers are looking for.

Market research can be conducted through a variety of formats, including surveys, personal interviews, focus groups, observations, and field trials. Surveys are the most commonly used method, and they're often considered the most powerful tool for conducting market research.

Consider the following types of surveys:
1) In-person surveys
In the past, this form of survey was used most frequently, and the results were quite effective. They can be conducted in real time, with fewer unknowns, at any location. They can also be run by experts who have the knowledge base to ask probing, intelligent questions. The surveyor can stimulate all five senses, which might be needed in certain cases. Respondents can touch, taste, and smell the product, then give a response. The reach of a surveyor in such cases is much higher, as they can get people who don't have access to the internet or are otherwise hard to access.

2) Telephonic surveys
For this method, surveyors contact respondents via phone. Surveyors are able to contact a defined sample of the population or acquire con-

tact data from companies suitable to a particular product. It's possible to reach a huge amount of population, as most of respondents have access to a telephone or a mobile phone. The drawback: since you can't see the person, it's difficult to ascertain their full response.

3) Mail surveys
As the name implies, in this type of survey, a prepared questionnaire is sent out to a sample population. Mail surveys are generally considered to be lower cost than telephonic surveys or in-person surveys, but they tend to have a very low response rate. The questionnaire is sent to the respondent's mailing address along with a prepaid envelope, so they can easily send the response back. The drawbacks: the response rate is low, so it isn't a very predictable source for taking surveys.

4) Online surveys
Nowadays, given our broad access to technology and its relevance, online surveys are the most common format. Many companies pay for respondents to fill out online surveys—you can easily sign up on websites like Swagbucks, InboxDollars, etc. and begin taking surveys. After filling in personal details and taking a basic questionnaire, the website saves your profile and starts sending you targeted surveys, and you're paid after they're completed.

However, market research and survey results are usually not exhaustive enough to prepare a business for making final decisions. We may be in a situation with multiple choices on the table and be unable to draw conclusions. Moreover, this type of data collection activity doesn't really help until you analyze the data in a way that leads to informed decisions. In such a scenario, we use a method called Backward Market Research (BMR).

BACKWARD MARKET RESEARCH

In 1985, Professor Alan R. Andreasen formulated the concept of BMR, and in so doing, he explained why most market research isn't actionable and doesn't lead us to a great outcome. He insisted that to have great results, we should start from where the research really ends, then work backward.

The BMR process:
1) Rather than defining the type of market research you want or the data you want to gather, **figure out the problem you want to solve.**

2) Once you know the problem, **define what the report should look like.**
3) This will lead to the data needed to build such a report. We then need to check: **does the data exist, or do we need to do some work to gather that data?**
4) Next, **design a plan to help you collect this data and do the analysis.**
5) **Perform the analysis.**
6) The data will then be available for your report, which will provide results and help solve your problem.

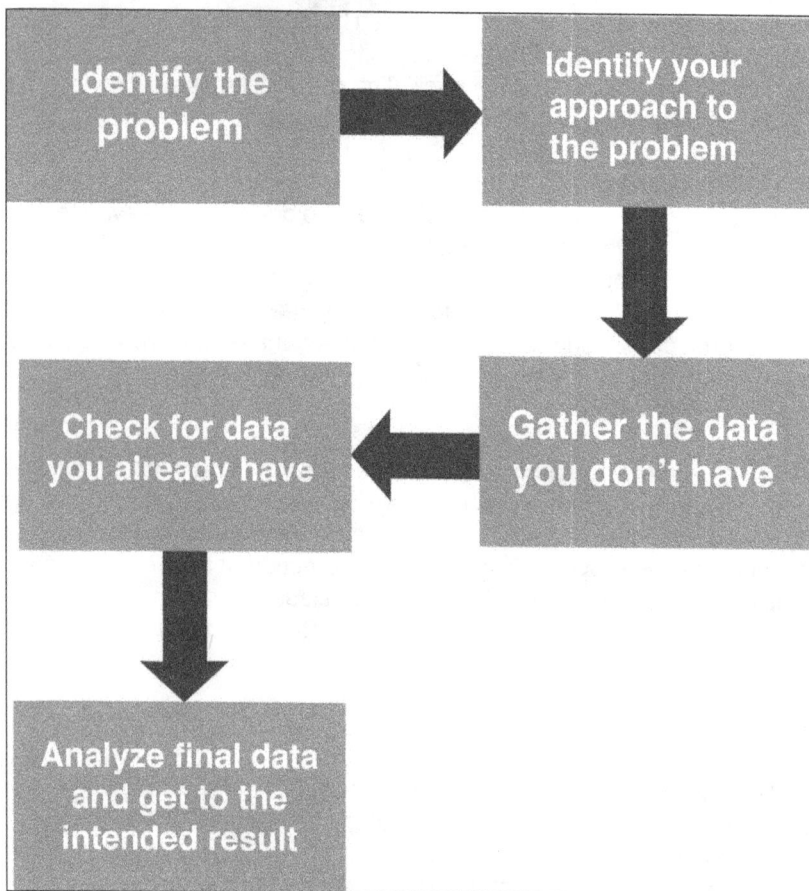

Let's check out the BMR approach through an example . . . imagine that our team is working for a chain that operates niche boutique hotels across five cities in the US. In the last year, we signed up with most travel websites and built our own application for our exclusive customers, but we've still noticed a drop in sales.

We need to come up with something new to get customers coming back to the hotel. Our team suggests a technological change—perhaps we need to add a few new features to the application to increase the occupancy rate.

Our market research offers a few interesting findings:
Background: An expensive boutique hotel in five different cities across the US
Age: 25–35
Gender: Male, 55%; Female, 45%
Income: USD 65,000–USD 125,000
Interests: Outdoors Activity, 55%; Clubbing, 75%
Marital status: Single, 85%; Married, 15%

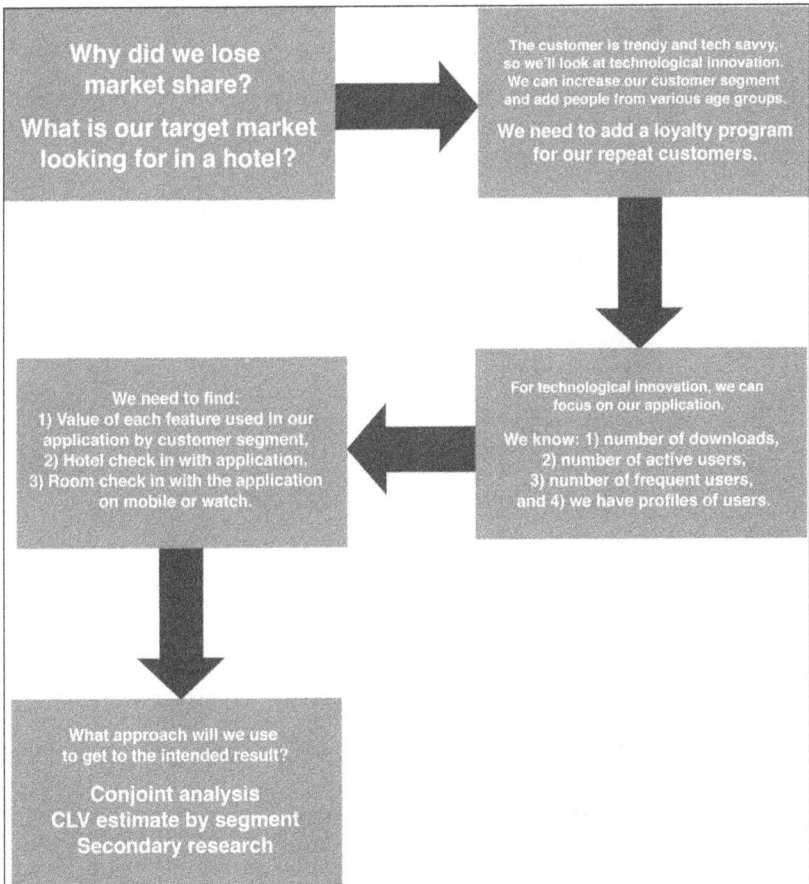

Cars: Luxury, 57%; Non-luxury, 43%
Technology Savvy: Yes, 83%; No, 17%
Customer profile: Young, trendy professionals who like technology and live in style; most of them are single and enjoy going out and having fun

Because we have knowledge about customer demographics from market research, we don't need further surveys or research to identify new features to add to our application. The BMR model will help us pinpoint the most effective new feature.

CONJOINT ANALYSIS

Conjoint Analysis is a statistical method used for market research activities. This type of analysis helps us find out how people value different features in products. We select a few features to measure, then analyze how changing the price of the product will have an effect on demand for the product in the market.

For example, let's take a look at a refreshing drink sold by top retailers. For this conjoint analysis, we'll indicate 1 = most preferred and 4 = least preferred.

In the table on the left, if both products are priced at $1.69, Gatorade is the most preferred brand. If priced at $2.69, Gatorade stays on top.

Gatorade	Store Brand		Gatorade	Store Brand	
1	3	$1.69	1	2	$1.69
2	4	$2.69	3	4	$2.69

In the table on the right, the situation changes—when the store brand is priced at $1.69, it's preferred more than the Gatorade priced at $2.69.

As we perform a conjoint analysis, we observe which brand is preferred at what price.

CUSTOMER LIFETIME VALUE (LTV)
ESTIMATE BY SEGMENT

The customer lifetime value (LTV) is the total amount of profit we make from a customer during the lifetime relationship we maintain with them.

Starbucks performed an illuminating case study on customer LTV to help maximize return on marketing dollars. In 2012, the company planned to open around 600 stores across the globe, and 25 percent of those stores in China. So, they picked up sales figures from 2004 to estimate customer LTV. Starbucks took steps to ensure they were calculating the right trends, particularly ones that would help them expand globally.

What variables would you consider important for your business model?

In the case of Starbucks, the important measurable variables for LTV were:
* **customer expenditure/visit**
* **number of visits per week**
* **avg. customer value/week**

After we calculate all the variables, we plug in the constant factors that apply for our business model.

Constant factors in the Starbucks business model:
* **T = Average customer life span** (how long someone remains a customer). For Starbucks, the average customer life span is twenty years.
* **R = Retention rate.** The percentage of customers who, over a given period of time, repurchase when compared to an equal and preceding period of time. Starbucks has a value of 75 percent.
* **P = Profit margin per customer.** For Starbucks, this is 21 percent.
* **I = Rate of discount.** The interest rate used in discounted cash flow analysis to determine the present value of future cash flows. For Starbucks, this is 10 percent.
* **M = Average gross margin per customer lifespan.** Starbucks has a profit margin of 21.3 percent (as per constant p). If the average customer spends $25,272 during their time as a customer (t), Starbucks's gross margin is $5,382.94.

CALCULATE LTV

Simple LTV (in the above example):
52(a) x t = 52 (24.30) x 20 = $25,272

Customer LTV Equation:
T(52 x s x c x p) = 20(52 x 5.90 x 4.2 x .213) = $5,489

Tradition LTV equation:

$$M\left(\frac{r}{1+i-r}\right) = 5382.94\left(\frac{.75}{1+.1-.75}\right) = \$11,535$$

Average LTV:
(Simple LTV + Customer LTV + Traditional LTV) / 3
(25272+5489+11535) / 3 = 42296 / 3 = $14,099

Don't think too hard about how many coffees you've had at Starbucks.
Photo by Taylor Franz on Unsplash

Now that Starbucks understands the average LTV of the customer, they have to spend less than $14,099 to acquire a new customer. However, if they're spending more than $14,099 per new customer, they'll lose money.

In this study, Starbucks went a step further and *segmented* customers on the basis of *average customers* and *good customers* by examining total purchases over a long period of time. The company then calculated the LTV of both segments.

Not all customers are equal—and it is important to know the benefits of spending more to acquire good customers.

It's usually smart to invest more to acquire good customers, instead of spending a lot to merely acquire average customers. In the case of a lending institution, one bad customer can erode the profit margin of ten average customers.

For Starbucks, the LTV of a good customer is $9,000, and the LTV of an average customer is $7,000. So, the difference in acquiring a good customer is around $2,000.

In addition, the study concluded that customer satisfaction boosts the LTV. Research has found that a 5 percent increase in customer retention can increase profits by 25 percent to 95 percent.

At Starbucks, the customer satisfaction rate is a whopping 89 percent.

SECONDARY RESEARCH

Secondary research is also known as the more self-explanatory "desk research." The data for secondary research can be sourced from any primary research done in the past or any marketing websites. Other secondary research sources might be old reports, surveys, and public resources, like libraries and government departments.

In the Starbucks example discussed above, we talked about customer segmentation, where customers were segmented into average and good customers.

Segmenting is essential—any and every business should be able to segment, target, and position their customers.

THE STP APPROACH

Segmenting, targeting, and positioning are the marketing techniques most widely used to understand and define a company's customers and to make better judgments about increasing market share. The whole value proposition can be viewed differently when all three elements have been defined and aligned with the business and products.

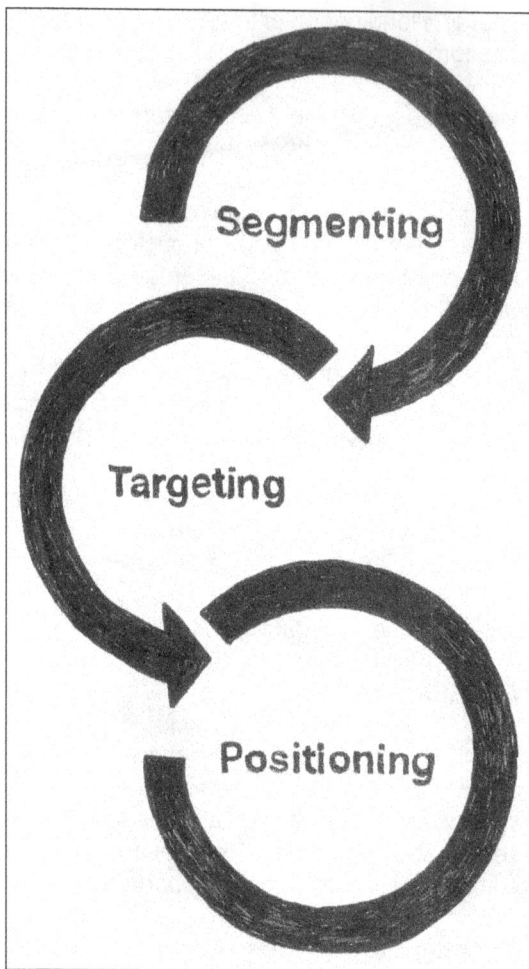

Any and every business must be able to effectively segment, target, and position their customers.

1) Segmenting

To segment customers into different groups, we look at similar characteristics, such as age, race, likes, and dislikes, so a group can be easily identified. Market segments should be distinctive: even if people in one group have similar needs, they should be different than people in another group in some way. As a guideline, we usually expect people in a similar segment to react similarly to a set of advertising or marketing techniques.

Chapter 8: Data-Based Decision Making

Let's imagine that we have three different sets of customers to sell our products to. In order to better identify their needs, we'll segment them according to characteristics that make them a closer match. Our business is a hotel chain, and we sell rooms to customers in the eighteen- to fifty-year-old age range, so we can segment customers according to their age groups.

We can further segment by the kinds of travelers that come to our hotel. Let's say we have student travelers, small business owners, corporate travelers, and families.

Based on segmentation, we can decide what kind of hotel properties and locations to invest in. If our hotel chain decides to stop catering to the student segment—the revenue coming from the student segment isn't as great as the others—then the hotel won't invest in properties in student towns. Instead, it would be preferable to invest in cities where corporations are firmly established and where people like to go for family vacations.

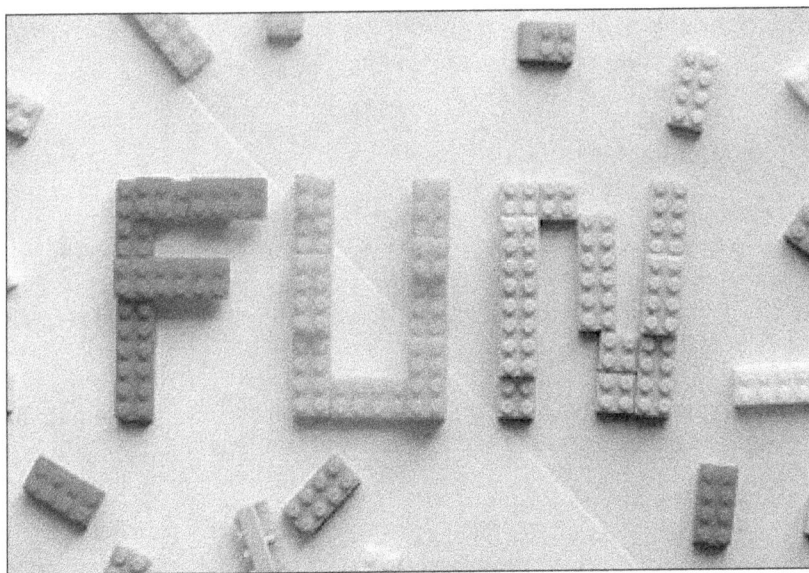

Reimagine an existing product for a new audience.
Photo by rawpixel on Unsplash

In 2012, the Lego Group, a Danish company that makes building block toys for children, posted a 25 percent increase in profits after launching Lego Friends, a series of toys designed for girls.[24] The product launch was conceived after dividing the children they catered to into various segments.

Lego not only segmented children by age but also by gender and character franchises. Their R&D results produced many ideas, including new brands and themes for different segments of children, all under the umbrella Lego brand. In the same year, more than 60 percent of Lego Group's sales were from new product launches. For girls, the Lego Friends theme—in which colors were given importance, as well as other activities tailored to girls—became a big hit.

2) Targeting

The next step in the STP process is targeting. Once we have segmented the customers, it's highly important to decide which customers to target. In the hotel chain example, will our company target students or corporate travelers?

The right segment to target should be:
- **measurable**
- **sustainable**
- **accessible**
- **differentiable**

As a Product Manager, it's crucial to understand marketing. You can think of marketing as oil for the machinery that Product Managers build. To determine the right target market, we need to evaluate the attractiveness of that target market for our situation and the advantages we'd have going into it.

Segmentation can help us further evaluate which group to target. To refine the search, we can select the basis of our segmentation.

Demographics	Age, income, location, channel features, performance
Behavior	Spending habits, application usage
Decision making	Power to make decisions, knowledge, competition, budget
Geographical	Location, climate, population, density

At this point, we need to understand the purpose of the product we're selling. For different people, the purpose behind the purchase of the same product may vary at different times.

For example, consider two customers who each take a personal loan. The product is similar but the two may have different needs. Customer A may want to consolidate debt on his credit cards, whereas Customer B may want to invest in a business. Another example is expensive chocolates: Customer A might be purchasing them to give as a gift, whereas Customer B might just be fond of consuming chocolate.

We can do a customer value analysis and competitive benchmarking to understand different kinds of customers and tailor our offerings to suit target customers.

Let's test the process of targeting for a hotel booking website. Here, we have three different types of customers:

- Cat-A—people who like to plan a holiday in advance (people with families and children)
- Cat-B—people who don't have time to plan in advance but who would like to go on a vacation when they can find the time
- Cat-C—people who travel for work

Key features	Customer value analysis Problems to be solved				Benchmarking with competition Competitive offering		
	Planned holiday	Unplanned holiday	Corporate travel	Hotels.com	Priceline	Hotwire	Orbitz
Full travel concierge	L	L	L	L	H	L	H
Type of property	H	H	H	H	L	L	H
Booking speed	L	H	H	H	L	H	H
Loyalty program	H	H	H	H	L	L	H
Customer service	H	L	L	L	H	H	H
Deals	H	H	L	L	H	H	L

As we can see above, Cat-A people are very concerned with the type of property they choose, are focused on the reward program and deals the website will offer, and need great customer service. Cat-B people are more concerned with the speed of booking and have less time to deal with customer service. Cat-C people have no time for engaging with customer service, as they're always on the go, but they value the property, rewards program, and speed of booking.

Hotels.com has a large list of properties, offers great speed of booking, and has an amazing rewards program. On the contrary, Hotwire doesn't let you choose the property and has no rewards program, but it does offer low and competitive pricing. To work effectively at each organization, it's important to understand the correct type of customer to target.

For Hotels.com, the target customers could be corporate travelers, as they fulfill all the important criteria. Should we also target Cat-A and Cat-B customers, for whom the value proposition is the highest? In this case, Hotels.com should target the Cat-B customers, who always travel unplanned—they're looking for the right property to choose from and the want speed of booking, plus a good rewards program.

3) Positioning

Sometimes we buy similar products at varied prices. The ideological purpose of the product could be the same, while the perception differs. We differentiate our products from competitors and create a persona for our product in the customer's mind through *brand position*. A good positioning strategy will help the brand create a unique image and stand out.

At a time when the world considered electric and hybrid vehicles to be small and less powerful, Tesla positioned itself as an electric sports car. Tesla avoided comparing itself to other electric or hybrid cars, like the Chevy Volt or the Toyota Prius, and created a new class of its own.

What's the competition in this picture? Think outside the airport . . .
Photo by Karl Magnuson on Unsplash

So, if a customer is interested in buying a sports car and values electric cars, the first brand that comes to mind is the Tesla.

Southwest Airlines is another classic example. When Southwest Airlines launched, they couldn't compete with large airlines like American, United, and Delta, so they targeted customers who wanted to fly smaller distances and save time.

Instead of choosing large airlines as a competitor, Southwest's first competition was road travel.

They initially launched smaller routes, like Dallas to San Antonio and Houston. Both were short hops: Dallas to San Antonio is 273 miles, and Dallas to Houston is 239 miles. For these routes, existing alternative were to drive or take a train. The company had chosen to differentiate their product based on speed. Next came convenience and cost of travel.

Southwest kept it simple and maintained very low prices. They always operated from smaller airports, which had low airport fees and thus made short travel easier and cheaper for their customers. These factors, plus many other initiatives, helped them achieve this unique brand position and established them as a successful brand.

In today's disruptive world, Product Managers handle targeting, segmenting, and positioning, but there's more. *It's also our role to take care of the strategic alignment of the product offering and keep it aligned with marketplace trends.*

In 2005, Professor Mauborgne and W. Chan Kim from INSEAD wrote a book called *Blue Ocean Strategy*. According to the authors, companies that compete in a red ocean are caught in a conventional approach— they're trying to beat the competition by lowering prices or giving value-added services to their existing product.

Companies that create a blue ocean don't need to use other companies as a benchmark to create their own products and services. Instead, they use the approach of value innovation. This capacity separates winners from losers in our contemporary environment.

Instead of focusing on beating the competition, companies need to focus on making the competition irrelevant—this is the crux of value innovation.

A profound example here is Cirque de Soleil, a Canadian street-performing company that morphed into high-end performers. A surprising fact: when Cirque de Soleil started to make this shift, both the circus industry (and most circus companies) were in a state of decline. People weren't interested in the form of entertainment, and there was a great deal of noise in the media about animal cruelty.

Cirque de Soleil went for a turnaround by basing their shows on themes like Michael Jackson and The Beatles and by choosing not to use animals in their productions. They became a big hit. The benchmark they created was different than any other company trying to compete with them, and at the same time, they made competition in the circus industry irrelevant.

4 DIFFERENTIATING PM SKILLS—VISION

9 Being Bold

> *"Fear doesn't make bad news go away.*
> *Fear makes bad news go into hiding."*
>
> — Richard Sheridan, CEO Menlo Innovations[27]

In 2009, Airbnb had launched multiple times and received national attention from the press, yet the company was close to going bust.[28] Revenues were down to $200 per week. Hardly anyone noticed their service, let alone took it seriously.

The team was determined to scale and kept trying to expand operations in order to drive more listings and grow revenue. Like most startups, they were preoccupied with creating a growth spike.

As Airbnb founder Brian Gretsky recounts, "We had this Silicon Valley mentality that you had to solve problems in a scalable way because that's the beauty of code . . . You can write one line of code that can solve a problem for one customer, 10,000 or 10 million. For the first year of the business, we sat behind our computer screens trying to code our way through problems."[29]

Y Combinator founder Paul Graham encouraged the founders to go back to the basics. He advised that it was perfectly okay to do things that don't scale. The founders took this to heart and worked on re-framing their problem.

After reviewing the data for listings in New York City, the team noticed a pattern: the listings had poor-quality images, often taken via cellphone or otherwise unprofessionally photographed. Customers weren't booking rooms online . . . because they couldn't see what they were getting.

The founders traveled to New York City, personally met with the hosts, and got to work as photographers. They provided each host with high-resolution pictures of their listings—and watched revenue almost double.

The Airbnb team learned that *their mindset was an obstacle*. As soon as they dropped the preconceived notion that all actions needed to be scalable, they were able to use a truly experimental mindset, and this helped them grow quickly.

Descaling helps you think clearly. Brian Chesky credits Paul Graham with giving the team "permission to do things that don't scale," and emphasizes that this one insight fundamentally altered Airbnb's future.

After we identify the right set of problems and prepare a good hypothesis for experimentation, solutions will eventually become scalable.

Most founders worry about revenue growth and base their feature decisions on pleasing VCs or other stakeholders. But following such conventional wisdom may blind you to opportunities all around.

Airbnb's story teaches us that a founding team needs to be gutsy, curious, and willing to treat your customer with the ultimate respect. These guys literally packed their bags, heaved themselves across the country, and tried their own product. In a continuation of this spirit, they allow every employee to do this in the first month at the company.

You don't have to be a founder to follow in their footsteps. *How will you try something different, experiment, and be bold?*

BOLD HUSTLE

Ryan Graves, the first hire at Uber, values hustle—in fact, he got his job by responding to a tweet from Uber's founder.[30] He jumped right in and got to work solving early-stage issues (at the time, it was difficult to get an Uber on weekends). By 2010, he was the company's CEO and had played a pivotal role in taking it to an over sixty-billion-dollar valuation.

Uber's ability to move at speed while experimenting with different versions of their mobile app has been crucial. By now, hustle as a core company value is a proven ingredient in its recipe for success.

MOONSHOTS

The next time you're stumped, take a step back.
Is there a different way to take a shot?
Photo by Fabian Oelkers on Unsplash

Astro Teller, the leader of Alphabet's research and development firm X, is widely recognized for employing moonshots as a strategy. In his view, 10x is easier than 10 percent.[31] This is true!

When we aim for incremental innovation, we often stick to the same old assumptions, methods, and tools. When you aim for 10x, we are suddenly forced to rely on bravery and creativity. This holds true not only for next-generation products like driverless cars or Hyperloop but also for more conventional businesses like ecommerce marketplaces.

It's common for development teams to wait for the Product Manager to provide a detailed set of directions. A 10x vision can be so inspiring that teams get excited to do the impossible and seek to empower themselves instead of holding back and waiting for guidance.

Many companies have instituted 20 percent unstructured time as a way to facilitate creative development. But as the pace of innovation has accelerated, both we and our teams *need to innovate every day*.

Moonshot thinking starts with picking a big problem: something huge, long-held, or global in scale. The next step is to articulate a radical solution—a solution that would solve the problem if it could somehow exist, even if the product or service sounds like it's straight out of a sci-fi story.

Finally, there should be some kind of concrete evidence showing that the proposed solution isn't quite as crazy as it seems—perhaps something that simply justifies a closer look. The evidence might mean a breakthrough in science, technology, or engineering that could make the solution possible within the next decade or so.

Gabor Forgacs, the co-founder of Modern Meadow, ate a pork chop that had been bio-printed by a special 3D printer designed for tissue engineering. That was a credible first step toward his company's moonshot goal. The next question is: how long will it take to get the price of the pork chop below those at the local grocery store? Moonshot!

Moonshots involve changing the nature of the question itself. As we've seen before in this book, Product Managers must be masters at both defining and reframing problems.

BOLD TIMING

Timing is a key component of boldness: it's not enough to be tenacious, we must also sense the right time to exit and win.

Zipcar had a humble beginning—the company started operations with just two cars and a few members and worked without any technology.[32] A member would simply walk to the front porch of her house, take the keys from underneath a pillow, open the glove compartment, and record the start time, end time, and odometer reading.

Robin Chase, the company's co-founder, worked hard to unlock the sharing economy through ongoing experiments. Her approach was to get in touch with the end customer as fast as possible, without worrying about the technology. Every time a company gets access to more money, data insights, or technology, it starts to do things that aren't focused on the customer—sometimes veering off in a completely wrong direction.

During the initial phase of Zipcar's launch, one of Chase's biggest learning moments was a pricing error. She realized that the pricing system she'd already released to customers had an error and that the company would need to increase rates by 25 percent to stay in business. Although she feared the consequences, she sent an email to all customers taking responsibility for the mistake, explaining how it had happened and that rates would have to increase—then steeled herself for the worst. Instead, many customers wrote back saying that they'd thought the prices seemed too low! Two customers wrote angry messages, and Chase called them to talk it over. The prices were successfully raised, and the company took off on a course of remarkable growth.

As Chase teaches us, we must be honest when things aren't going right, and work to fix them as directly and quickly as we can.

Zipcar received $75,000 in early-stage capital from angel investors. Per press release of Zipcar January 2013, Avis acquired Zipcar for approximately 500 million. Chase had successfully built and sold a giant car-sharing company.

FEARLESS

Lastly, being bold means being fearless. There will be times when your pursuit of an idea turns out to be not quite worth the investment. Or, you may find that you've been on a wrong path altogether. But being fearful will only hide bad news.

As a product leader, our foremost responsibility is to pump fear out of the room! Instead of hiding the information, be the first to embrace it. Start to develop a new momentum as a way to influence and encourage the right attention and decisions.

Sally works as a Product Manager (her name has been changed for privacy), and she runs one of the largest lines of products for an insurance distribution company. Her team was frustrated because a supplier file format had consistent, ongoing bugs. The supplier used to go out with the CIO of the company, and the two were still close pals. Sally had two options: let the bugs slide as long as possible or face her fears and discuss the situation.

Sally chose to start reporting on the bug data, and she exposed the severity of the problems her team was facing due to the supplier's unfinished product. The head of business, who paid close attention to the report, took action and called the CIO. A meeting was arranged with the supplier, and the issue came forward front and center.

As a result, the supplier moved their entire team to Sally's office for three weeks until every bug was fixed. They also took precautions to introduce a self-healing capability in their software. Sally is still with her company and has a bright career ahead.

This might seem like a small example of being fearless, but each step toward facing fears equips us to handle the next, potentially bigger task. People who fear losing their job due to speaking the truth are far more likely to get fired than those who are bold and willing to invite constructive conversation.

10 Managing Products in the Age of Self-Driving Cars

"If you want to do something new, you have to stop doing something old."

— Peter Drucker, Business Visionary

More often than not, Product Owners—or in our context, Product Managers—disagree with this statement: *the Product Owner is the CEO*.

If you disagree, your perspective is no less right. But to really be an effective Product Manager, you need to start making an internal shift to match to this statement.

We often hear this rebuttal, "As a Product Manager, I don't get to set the price. The decision is made above my pay grade or by a different department." And this might be the case. However, a Product Manager should be responsible for the profit and loss related to their product, so they need to *think about price as a precondition*, not as a post-condition.

The next argument goes, "I don't have a budget, so I don't have authority. My team doesn't report to me." This is true! Nothing you do will change this. However, look at high-performing Product Managers—they're super aligned to company strategic priority. They may not control the purse, but they influence how the dollars are spent and the type of engineering team they want in place. They're not autocratic CEOs, but by using influence and being aligned with company strategy, they work within their means to see their vision and expectations realized.

So, why would we call a Product Manager a CEO? Just like the CEO, who is advised by their team of experts, a Product Manager is advised by their own team, including engineers, quality control, and designers. The PM needs to listen to other points of view while doing what's right for the team and the customer. Their sole job is to formulate and aim for outcomes, determine what metrics help drive growth, and evaluate how they can influence metrics and factors to enable growth.

The final decision-making authority rests with the Product Manager. The hierarchy a Product Manager operates in may choose to override or make decisions on behalf of the Product Manager, depending on the stakes or maturity of the organization. Product Managers who have consistent empowerment issues may get demotivated quickly, which will influence the team. Ideally, higher management should provide the goals, then get out of the way of the Product Development team, enabling them to independently define the how. Ceremonies like sprint reviews can provide insight into the team's capabilities and allow for reset or tuning as needed.

Empowerment is a journey. Few Product Managers start here. *Earning credibility and respect of the team and leadership takes time.*

Every Product Manager needs to develop *presence*. This versatile quality is at the root of both leadership, strategy, and the capacity for action. Presence empowers the Product Manager to cascade strategies to their teams and colleagues with ultimate clarity. It helps them remain calm and focused in times of ambiguity and change. And it helps them inspire teams when they need to creatively demonstrate outcomes and achieve greater outcomes with less output.

Being centered allows the Product Owner to go beyond the product, to think more deeply about the customer. Even the most customer-oriented companies sometimes miss the essence of customer needs and edge cases that could hurt.

Let's take an example from Facebook: a friend posted to her Facebook account on the anniversary of her father's death. Facebook's feature on memories from the past reminded her with the "share" icon. While the intent of sharing memories is often great, a greater degree of emotional intelligence helps us discern that some memories are better off not shared. Code can't really distinguish good from the bad. This situation has a potential to get even worse with the advent of artificial intelligence. AI recognizes patterns and writes its own new code logic or algorithms. On the other hand, these algorithms can now read words like "RIP" or see crying icons or "sorry" and avoid recommending them in your memories section.

A friend's nine-year-old plays a game called Slither.io on her iPad. She always chooses to play against artificial intelligence instead of another person. When we asked her why she wants to play with a computer program versus another human being, she replied, "I trust the computer program more than the human being, and they will never get inside my iPad and do bad things! The artificial intelligence mode will always be nice to me."

The next generation of children has been exposed to advancing levels of artificial intelligence, and it's important for us to keep them in mind while designing products. A friend casually joked, "I'm not worried about the kids playing games with AI, but more worried when they grow up to twenty-five years old and come home one day to inform me they will marry a human-looking AI!"

When designing products like SIRI, Alexa, and other automatic computer-controlled products, there's a big question we'd like to ask in this vein: *how might AI represent this child's interest over the interests of her family or the greater society? Who will it serve?*

We're reminded of a scene from the movie *Terminator 2: Judgment Day*—and it suggests a future we could well come across. In the film, Sarah Connor reflects on the relationship between her son and the Terminator. She muses, "[The Terminator] would never leave him, and it would never hurt him, never shout at him, or get drunk and hit him, or say it was too busy to spend time with him. It would always be there. And it would die, to protect him." She realizes that the Terminator is more of a father to her son than any man had been or perhaps could ever be. In the future, will we prefer AI to others of our own kind?

Let's use what we've learned so far and try a case study on driverless cars. Our new vision is to make driverless cars safer than cars driven by people by a margin of over 99.9 percent.

At the outset, we note that in 2013, there were nearly ten million car accidents in the United States, so this is a major problem.

Causes of road accidents via DMV statistics (in order of priority):
1) Distracted driving: the result of a driver is trying to do multiple things while driving a car—for example, talking on the phone or responding to a text
2) Speeding: the second-greatest cause of road accidents
3) Drunk driving or driving under the influence
4) And more (but we'll release these in the future version of our product)

But wait, since the new car is driverless, it would automatically eliminate the above scenario and increase safety, right?

Well, let's take another look . . . it might eliminate distracted driving by humans, but what new safety concerns will come up with driverless cars?

We need to consider potential new scenarios:
1) Roads shared by both driverless cars and cars with human drivers—for example, planning for scenarios when human drivers don't signal a lane change
2) Software glitch that wasn't caught during testing, which later causes a car to fail and crash
3) Crosswalks for humans where actions are unpredictable and the chances of an accident where someone gets hit from behind are high
4) The reverse scenario, where a driverless car is following the rules and stops at a crosswalk that is busy and has a lot of people crossing—a typical driver would start inching into the crosswalk, but a driverless car would frustrate the humans behind it

And more . . .

Many companies investing in driverless car products followed these basic product development principles. They video-recorded many drivers over thousands of hours and created scenarios that eventually became patterns for self-driving cars.

For the purposes of our case study, this is how everything was broken down into the current version of the product being built:

1) **Driver interface:** though the cars are called "self-driving," this interface allows the driver to take over the controls when needed.

2) **Road safety:** an evolving intelligent software learns from city driving conditions—like construction work, safety speed limits, joggers, and bikers—and interfaces with the core driving module to adjust as necessary. This module parks your car or halts at a safe location based on the current driving conditions. It also learns from a regularly updated universal rules feed that makes the car smarter.

3) **Core driving module:** this program controls all mechanical controls in the car, along with the internals, such as air conditioning or heat. It controls the headlights, wipers when raining, and core driving on the road.

4) **External sensors and interface:** thousands of sensors are built into the cars, and all of these have fail safes. The sensor data is fed to modules, like the core driving module or road safety. The external sensor module constantly predicts road conditions and the need to accelerate, slow down, turn, stop, or even park.

5) **Fuel or gas:** not all cars are electrical, and some in the initial phases will need manual intervention for fueling or recharge.

6) **Mapping interfaces:** every possible drivable and walkable area needs to be mapped.

7) **Bonus options:** car manufacturers may offer self-driving cars for Uber, Lyft or other companies that operate passenger pick-up and drop-off service platforms.

Now that we've laid out a set of hypothetical modules, let's think about exploring this case further. For example, how would we build an MVP for each module?

How can we learn quickly?

11 Product Vision

"[Twitter's] strength has been in its speed and immediacy. Now the challenge is for Dorsey . . . to turn that strength into a success story."

— Erin Griffith[33]

Every Product Manager must deploy tools to ensure top-down alignment on an ongoing basis. These tools must deliver results that are *simple and unforgettable.*

In order to arrive at a simplified vision to unify and direct your team, you may choose to dig deeper:

- Who is your target customer?
- What needs do you want to serve for them?
- What value will your features provide them and at what cost?

A simple one-line statement that reminds your team why they exist is sufficient. Here's an example of a simple vision statement from Square, "Start accepting credit card payments anywhere with your smartphones." Notice that it's bold, simple, and measurable.

Product vision can contribute to a company's success . . . or failure. In the case of Google Glass, the target customer and the reasoning behind the product were both unclear. It was the company's first foray into wearables technology. The product was introduced to developers first, and in secretive ways, to a wider audience. Google had intended to learn about the purpose of the product during the launch, but post-launch, this vision was quickly diluted.[34] Security concerns were highlighted, customers received traffic tickets for using the product while driving, and the company decided to put a hold on the product until its target use could be defined and focused.

In 2006, GoPro, also a San Francisco-based company, introduced the Hero, a wearable digital camera, much like Google Glass. GoPro launched the product as a tool to enable athletes—anyone from terrain bikers to surfers and extreme skiers—to make professional-quality sports videos.

The company had a tightly defined mission: to improve the experience of sports enthusiasts by providing a professional-caliber tool not otherwise available.[35] It tapped into the hunger within the market for excellent, shareable images, and it created the ease of sharing a product feature.

Although the Hero lacked the minimal aesthetic of Google Glass, it was an instant hit.

GoPro tailored its product to the needs of a specific target market.

Chapter 11: Product Vision

12 Product Box

---

*"Alone we can do so little;
together we can do so much."*

— Helen Keller[36]

To encourage creativity while engaging your team, stakeholders, and even customers, consider playing an innovation game.[37] Play has the potential to encourage your team to make connections that might be stifled in a more narrowly defined work environment.

One particularly powerful game to stoke the fires of product development is called *product box*. Here, the goal is to create a cereal box version of your product.

A cereal box is a simple construction. It has plenty of space to convey what your product does—and the obvious space constraints encourage your brevity and creativity.

To begin, come together as a team and put everything your product will do on a product box. Present the content clearly, and make it attractive enough to pitch to a VC or internal customer. Then, see what feedback you receive. This process helps teams level up their vision of product development in a unique way.

The box isn't a throwaway artifact. Instead, it will help your team design a home page for the product.

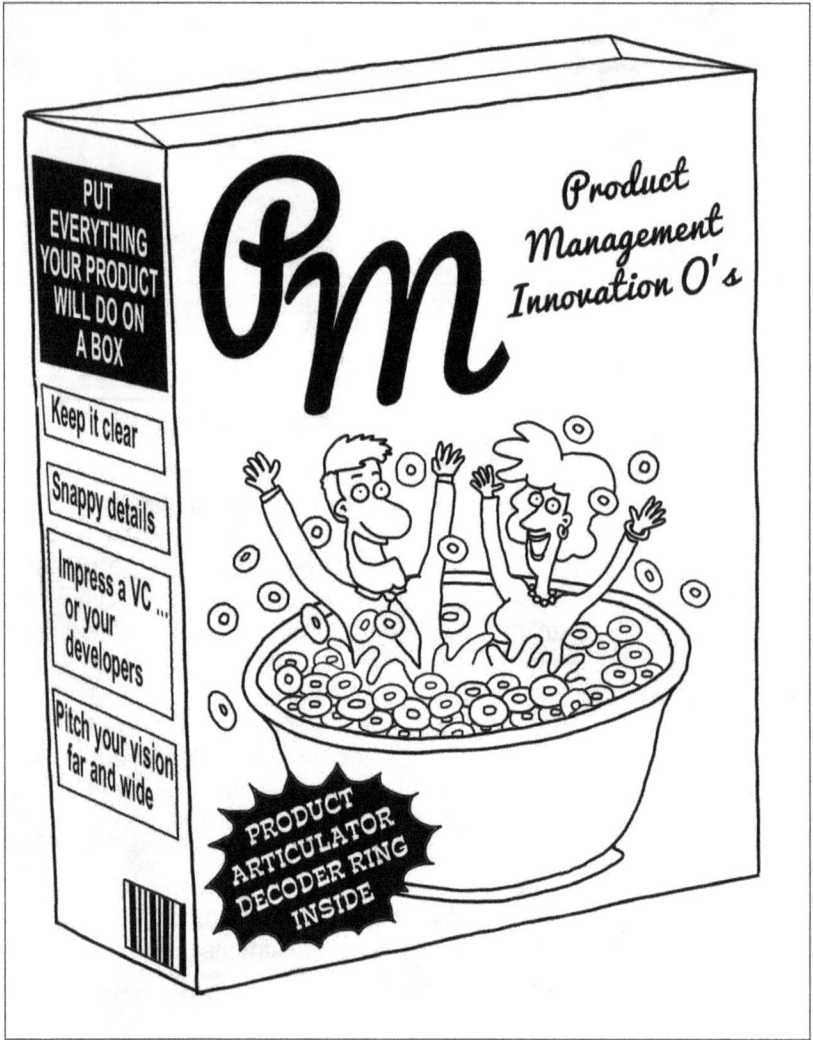

Let's go back to our example on Square, the credit card reader.[38] The vision for the product was simple: be able to accept payments almost anywhere.

To turn this vision into a product box, we might imagine the front of the box as a key image—perhaps the reader and a credit card—with the product tagline and value proposition.

The left side of the box might have detail specs on features—for example, a picture of someone swiping a card on the device—or information on broad features like security, signature, and pricing. The back of the box could be reserved for more advanced versions. Some teams prefer to create a different product box for each variation.

Continue refining your box so you can pitch your product idea in a short time, ideally, less than a minute. Every developer on your team should be able to pitch the box to stakeholders. This will ensure that everyone understands the vision.

How would you design a product box for your product?

5 DIFFERENTIATING PM SKILLS— STRATEGY

13 The Art of Letting Go

> "Nothing focuses your mind quite like flying a jet. That's one reason NASA requires that astronauts fly T-38s: it forces us to concentrate and prioritize in some of the same ways we need to in a rocket ship."
>
> — Chris Hadfield[39]

Slack achieved a one-billion-dollar valuation within just a few years of its founding.[40] Whether you use its platform or not, the company's rise is a fascinating case study.

Before Slack, teams used all kinds of different ad hoc services to coordinate their work—email chains, WhatsApp, or Google Hangouts messaging, and even text threads. Slack created a new product category: a dedicated messaging platform laser-focused on facilitating communication inside teams.

Like Facebook, where users view their feed multiple times a day, Slack designed its channels to be virtual lounges where team members could hang out all day and create brilliant stuff together. The company wanted the product to be vital and compelling, as if to say: if you're not on a Slack channel for your team's discussion, you're missing out on all the important stuff.

Slack originated from the ashes of an online gaming company called Glitch. The founder of Glitch (and later Slack) had wanted to build a gaming community that played without stopping. While the gaming component failed, its underlying concept became Slack's secret sauce. Many lessons from Glitch were rekindled in Slack—including a 24/7 on-line community feel, sense of fun, ease of use, and a light environment conducive to teamwork.

To launch one of its first versions, the Slack team used a media blitz to invite people to try Slack. On the first day, nearly 8,000 people joined and the team was delighted. Within a few weeks, over 15,000 people were actively using Slack—which *really* excited the team, because it indicated both adoption and spread. Slack had stumbled into a product market fit.

Product market fit (PMF) is no small matter.[41] According to Marc Andreessen, "Product market fit means *being in a good market with a product that can satisfy that market.*"[42] All too often, the focus is only on the latter and not the former.

Market strength is like the tide in that there's no sense in launching your ship when the tide is out. If you have a competent team and a decent product, a strong market will pounce on your product. But no matter how fantastic your team and product, if the market is fundamentally weak, sales will be slow and hard-fought.

> *"You can always feel when product market fit isn't happening. The customers aren't quite getting value out of the product, word of mouth isn't spreading, usage isn't growing that fast, press reviews are kind of 'blah,' the sales cycle takes too long, and lots of deals never close. And you can always feel product/market fit when it's happening. The customers are buying the product just as fast as you can make it—or usage is growing just as fast as you can add more servers."[43]*
> — Marc Andreessen

Slack had a sense from its metrics that they'd touched on a product market fit, but the concept goes beyond any one metric. There's no easy number that announces it, and you might not quite realize it in the moment. Instead, pay attention to the overall signs, just as Andreesen says: are sales dribbling or pouring in, are you having a hard time getting the word out, or are reporters calling to ask questions about the buzz around your product?

How did Slack get to the point where new users rushed to sign up by the thousands? As a dedicated reader of this book, you might have a guess . . .

Yep, that's right.

From the beginning, *Slack rigorously listened to their users.*

In its earliest stages, Slack invited teams to use the platform for free, just to get feedback on the product. They also recognized that their customers weren't individuals or companies, but product development teams within companies.

Slack absorbed feedback, rapidly iterated on features that worked, and kept updating their web and mobile platform. Then, they invited more teams and continued the iterations. The Slack development team actively sought customer feedback and reviews every day, through every conversation, and carefully prioritized the backlog.

For example, reducing email was often mentioned as a customer goal. One company had a massive internal list, and employees used it to communicate with over a thousand people inside the company. Of course, the emails were usually relevant for only a few people. Slack realized that providing global channels (such as #general) where people could chat about anything added to the product's appeal.

Globally displaced teams asked for snooze notifications on their mobile devices to prevent notifications at all hours. The Slack team built in these features very quickly based on user feedback and kept prioritizing their backlog—and they still maintain the rigor of this approach even today. Development teams inside Slack's offices have been using their own product and relentlessly improving their product as a result.

Stewart Butterfield, Slack's founder, articulated a sentiment comment among many founders: "There are industry-standard numbers, no doubt. But at the end of the day, only you can really determine your company's magic numbers—the numbers that shed light on who is really using your product (and how you can get them to keep using it)."[44]

Over time, the Slack team discovered that their magic number is 2,000 messages, the equivalent of a full week of messages between team members. Steward Butterfield says, "Based on experience of which companies stuck with us and which didn't, we decided that any team that has exchanged 2,000 messages in its history has tried Slack—really tried it."[45]

Crucially, once a team had tried Slack, they stayed. Butterfield continued, "Regardless of any other factor, after 2,000 messages, 93% of those customers are still using Slack today." The ones that really try it out, stick with it.

At each stage, the Slack team focused on the features most vital to their product vision. *And they didn't cut corners to achieve them.*

For Slack, the three most important features were:
1) Search
The Slack team knew that users expect to find what they're looking for quickly, so speed would be an important factor for user adoption. As Butterfield said, "People need to feel confident that when they read a document or conversation, they don't have to worry about labeling or storing it—that they'll be able to find it again later if and when they need it." Google has set the standard in this category, and users have high expectations. Disappointing expectations for search speed and efficiency can be fatal.

2) Synchronization
The Slack team surveyed competing platforms and carefully made note of areas for improvement and pain points. Butterfield said, "One of the things that drove us nuts about every other internal platform was that it was very difficult to pick up in the same place when you switched devices—say, when you left your laptop and picked something back up on your phone." To evolve beyond competitors, from the outset, Slack featured "leave-state synchronization." Each time a user leaves a conversation, the point they've reached is saved, so they can pick up seamlessly on different devices.

3) Simple file-sharing
Slack offers file-sharing through simple, integrated features designed to enhance productivity. It's easy to drag and drop files into the messaging stream. Files from popular services like Google Docs and Dropbox are compatible, and Slack also integrates sharing permissions from outside services.

Excellent attention to its user experience adds up, especially for a software platform designed to be used constantly. The combination of many, many tiny gains and improvements has catapulted the company to a status far above its competition.

On its own, each feature doesn't seem like much. They're not particularly dazzling, and most of them don't reinvent the wheel. But in combination and when tailored exactly to the needs of a great market through iterative feedback, the overall product proved to be a game-changer.

> *"We had a lot of conversations about choosing the three things we'd try to be extremely, surprisingly good at. . . . And ultimately we developed Slack around really valuing those three things. It can sound simple, but narrowing the field can make big challenges and big gains for your company feel manageable. Suddenly you're ahead of the game because you're the best at the things that really impact your users."[46]*
> — Stewart Butterfield

Another example of great product market fit is the streaming device company called Roku. In 2016, Roku grew their share of the smart TV market in the US to over 13 percent, and customers streamed more than nine billion hours of video and music.[47]
Before Roku, trying to stream movies off the internet was a complicated maneuver, requiring different sorts of cables and devices. Roku packaged this messy experience and simplified it into one product: a set-top box that allows you to stream movies from your Netflix queue directly onto your TV.

Streaming performance is excellent—with no sputtering, excellent audio quality, and near-DVD-caliber video. If you stop watching a film and come back to it later, an auto-bookmark is created, providing the option to resume viewing right where you left off.

The company has grown quickly and established itself as a competitor to massive companies like Amazon and Apple. Nonetheless, it will be a battle to grow and innovate its product offering in the face of intense competition.

GROWTH HACKING

Growth hacking is a term coined by Sean Ellis. In essence, it means *run multiple tests to determine the right problem and solution, then keep scaling the tests to achieve growth.* The growth-hacking principle is based on quick, cheap, and simple tests to either prove or invalidate each hypothesis.

To explain growth hacking, we'll use a non-tech story. Back in 1996, Britain's cycling team was ranked number 17 in the world and had just won two bronze medals at the Olympic Games in Atlanta, Georgia. Not bad, right? The team was world-class and had represented Britain on the Olympic podium. Other folks might have called it a day.

Enter the transformative coaching of Sir David Brailsford. His approach: break down every aspect of riding a bike and improve it by one percent.

By 2012, the British cycling team ranked first in the world, and British riders had won 12 medals (including eight gold) at the London Olympic Games. How did they achieve this astonishing growth?

It wasn't magic. It was a long, slow, relentless series of micro, cost-effective, and human-centered optimizations that were effectively scaled. This is what a growth hacking mindset looks like, and these are the kinds of results it can achieve.

Qualities of a good growth hacker:
1) **Mindset**—growth hackers focus on accelerated growth on a minimum budget. It's all about users (or an alternative KPI, depending on your business).
2) **Curiosity and creativity**—don't get fixated on spending a particular budget. Go back to basics, and think about tapping into human behavior (remember, we're social animals).

3) **Internal culture**—the business needs to be open to experimentation, and inevitably, some ideas will fail.
4) **Balanced team**—the team should include marketers with a broad knowledge base and capabilities in both "left brain" and "right brain" disciplines. Marketers should be both analytical and data driven yet at the same time, understand brands, storytelling, and experiential marketing.
5) **Team mindset**—one individual person is unlikely to have all the skills needed for growth-focused marketing. Individuals should excel in coordination with their team.

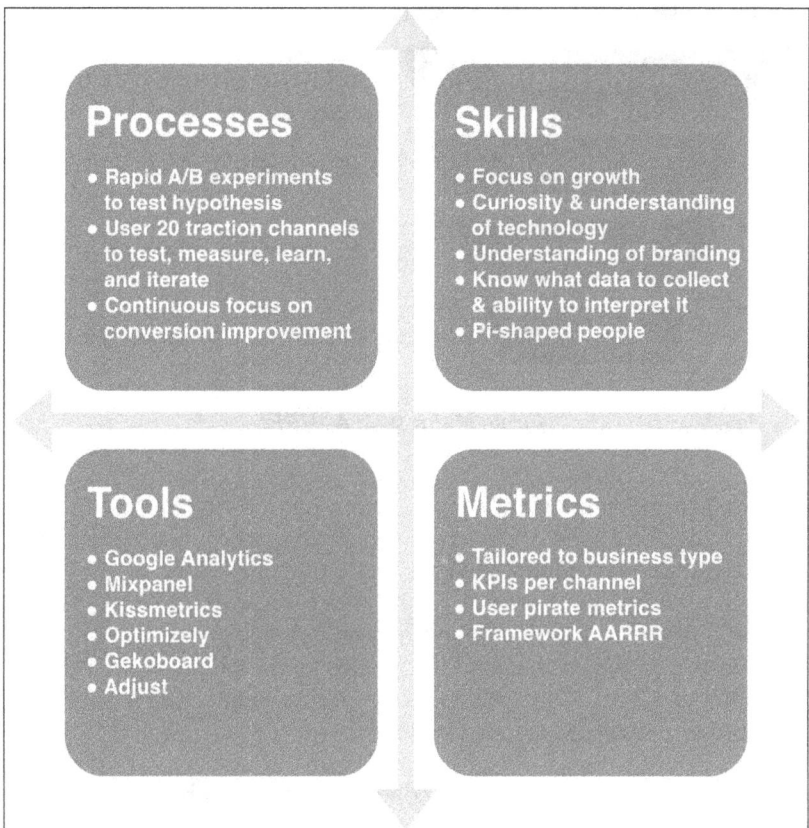

Processes
- Rapid A/B experiments to test hypothesis
- User 20 traction channels to test, measure, learn, and iterate
- Continuous focus on conversion improvement

Skills
- Focus on growth
- Curiosity & understanding of technology
- Understanding of branding
- Know what data to collect & ability to interpret it
- Pi-shaped people

Tools
- Google Analytics
- Mixpanel
- Kissmetrics
- Optimizely
- Gekoboard
- Adjust

Metrics
- Tailored to business type
- KPIs per channel
- User pirate metrics
- Framework AARRR

Just as the British cycling team broke down every single step of their race and worked to improve it through multiple optimizations, internet companies need to study their traffic funnel and break it down into how a user's journey really takes place.

What are the points of friction, and how can they be rigorously reduced? Amazon's buy-with-one-click is a great example of optimized buying flow with nearly all friction removed. Likewise, Amazon Go is a checkout-free store, which again eliminates nearly any chance of friction.

Investor Dave McClure of 500 Hats has often spoken about the marketing funnel and startup metrics for Pirates (AAARR). This is a useful tool for all types of organizations.

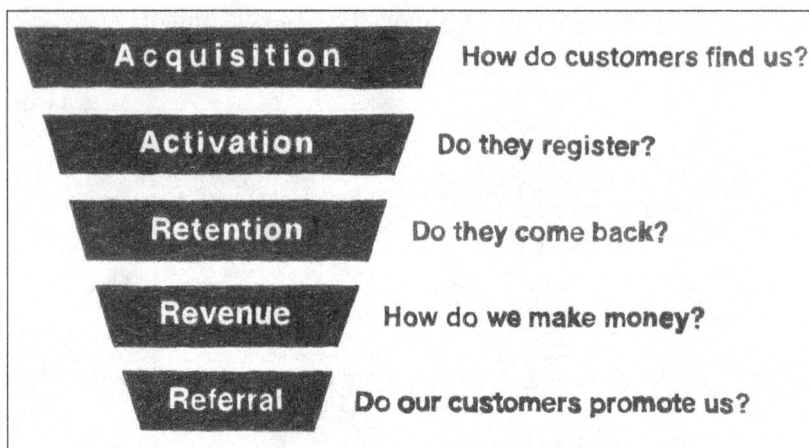

Acquisition	How do customers find us?
Activation	Do they register?
Retention	Do they come back?
Revenue	How do we make money?
Referral	Do our customers promote us?

Pirate Metrics . . . AARRR!

Metrics like monthly or daily active users can be helpful, but to really analyze the conditions under which users return to your app or platform, you'll need to run a cohort analysis.

Cohort analysis is a tool for identifying and studying engagement problems versus growth problems.[48] If you have an existing product, we highly recommend cohort analysis to see if your new user base is continuing to return and engage with your platform.

Let's walk through the steps of a cohort analysis. As an example, imagine that we have an app, and we'd like to analyze user engagement. We start by constructing a cohort of users who launched our app for the first time and revisited the app in the next ten days.

App Launched ↓   % Active users after App Launches →

Cohort	Users	Day 0	Day 1	Day 2	Day 3	Day 4	Day 5	Day 6	Day 7	Day 8	Day 9	Day 10
Jan 25	1,098	100%	33.9%	23.5%	18.7%	15.9%	16.3%	14.2%	14.5%	*Retention over user lifetime*		12.1%
Jan 26	1,358	100%	31.1%	18.6%	14.3%	16.0%	14.9%	13.2%	12.9%	*lifetime*		
Jan 27	1,257	100%	27.2%	19.6%	14.5%	12.9%	13.4%	13.0%	10.8%	11.4%		
Jan 28	1,587	100%	26.6%	17.9%	14.6%	14.8%	14.9%	13.7%	11.9%			
Jan 29	1,758	100%	26.2%	20.4%	16.9%	14.3%	12.7%	12.5%				
Jan 30	1,624	100%	26.4%	18.1%	13.7%	15.4%	11.8%					
Jan 31	1,541	100%	23.9%	19.6%	15.0%	14.8%						
Feb 01	868	100%	24.7%	16.9%	15.8%							
Feb 02	1,143	*Retention over product lifetime*		18.5%								
Feb 03	1,253	*lifetime*										
All Users	13,487	100%	27.0%	19.2%	15.4%	14.9%	14.0%	13.3%	12.5%	13.1%	12.2%	12.1%

From the above retention table, we can infer the following: 1,358 users launched an app on January 26. Day 1 retention was 31.1 percent, Day 7 retention was 12.9 percent, and Day 9 retention was 11.3 percent. So, on the seventh day after using the app, one in eight users who launched the app on January 26 were still active users.

Out of all the new users during this time (13,487 users), 27 percent were retained on Day 1, 12.5 percent on Day 7, and 12.1 percent on Day 10.

Product lifetime (as depicted vertically down the table): Comparing different cohorts at the same stage in their life cycle, we can see what percentage of people in a cohort are coming back to the app after three days, and so on. The early lifetime months can be linked to the quality of your onboarding experience and the performance of customer success team.

User lifetime (as depicted horizontally to the right of the table): Seeing the long-term relationship among people in any cohort, we can ascertain how long users are coming back and how strong or how valuable that cohort is. This can be presumably linked to something like the quality of the product, operations, and customer support.

Whatever key metrics you define for your business, cohort analysis lets you view how the metrics develop over the customer lifetime and the product lifetime.

Cohort analysis enables you to not only view which customers leave and when but also helps you understand why—so you can fix it. It's an essential tool for identifying how well users are being retained and for determining the primary factors driving growth, engagement, and revenue for your app.

6 DIFFERENTIATING PM SKILLS—TEAM

14 Good Product Development Teams— Myth or Reality?

"Good teams become great ones when the members trust each other enough to surrender the ME for the WE."[49]

— Phil Jackson

Let's imagine for a moment that we have an inspiring, actionable, and altogether revolutionary vision to make driving safe. Whether our idea involves a car, plane, or the elimination of cars by teleportation devices—one way or another—we'll need a team to help achieve our vision.

We were once asked a question at a conference: why is Product X our favorite, compared to Product Y? We'd heard this question before, and in reply, we said: we trust the team that builds Product X, and *they trust each other*. The Product X team is fully oriented around solving issues for their customers. As customers, we know we're front and center in all discussions with the Product X team.

On the other hand, the team that builds Product Y doesn't have this mindset, and we can tell by the feature releases and structure of the product itself. It just isn't oriented toward the customer in the same way.

In fact, just by using a product, one can sense the qualities of the team behind it—and how close-knit or alienated they are.

Nokia achieved worldwide acclaim for its hardware. However, the company's development process was dominated by hardware engineers. Simultaneously, software experts were seen as less valuable and their contributions underestimated.

Leadership at Apple viewed both hardware and software as equal elements of a successful product, and they *encouraged employees to form multidisciplinary design teams.*

Nokia went from raking in 50 percent of all profits in the mobile-phone industry in 2007 to barely clinging to a 3 percent share of the global handset market by 2010. Apple's holistic approach to smartphone design had delivered a decisive blow to its competitor.

A massive loss in market share—down in the case of Nokia and up in the case of Apple—was the result of each company's approach to forming and valuing teams.

SCALING TEAMS, NOT HEADCOUNTS

Scaling up introduces its own set of issues. The shift from one team to twenty teams, then to 100 teams, inevitably places stress on company structures. By way of example: a mid-size company won a large, multi-hundred-million-dollar contract. In response, the company immediately turned to hiring, and 500 job offers were released in the first week alone.

Within two months, the company swelled with over 2,000 new hires. Within six months, it became clear that hiring compromises (quality of engineers, language compatibility, cultural fit, and more) had caused irreparable damage to team formation. Despite the fact that best-in-class leaders had been deployed to handle the new contract buildout, the failure was catastrophic—and no amount of money could come to the rescue.

Many thought leaders talk about forming rich, cross-functional teams. While this is often a great vision, in practice, most companies find changes in structure to be intensely challenging. The stress of change eventually kills all change efforts within a given company.

Breaking down silos using teams is a very powerful and effective means to gain speed, but this action must be approached delicately, as it will always be politically charged. Nobody likes to lose power.

Whether we are successful in breaking down the silos or not, *one consistent principle is that groups should be divided into smaller teams.* Amazon's team formation definition bears repeating: "If you can't feed a team with two pizzas, it is too large." As a best practice, this limits team size to fewer than ten people.

What's wrong with larger teams? Simply put, it becomes too difficult for everyone to see and connect with value while contributing to the greater good of the team.

At one company, an internal tools team had seven people. They were well-divided between functions, and their goal was to provide a scalable toolset for the organization to collaborate within. The team had metrics, including a number of Slack messages, JIRA comments,[50] and healthy conversations to define the right portfolio of products. The team roles were divided into: the Product Owner, who aligned the backlog for the team based on the vision for the team and strategic priorities; the functional manager, who doubled up as leader and process coach while also handling management responsibilities; four developers, who also knew details of the systems administration; and one tester. This team nailed every outcome they set as a team.

A year later, after a new VP-level leadership shift, a more positive focus for growing the collaboration tools team was set in motion. Seven more developers were hired to help build a new portfolio management toolset internal to the company. Within two months of growing the team, the lead developer quit and moved to another company. The Product Owner also moved on to another part of the company. Three other senior developers started to look for active opportunities outside the team. On follow-up discussions with the team members, it was uncovered while the executive priorities of this team had grown and they'd loved this, they had also lost something very crucial: *how each of them contributed value to the greater good of the team.* Everyone was searching for a place within the team and spending a tremendous amount of time in role clarity. This example shows how a very high-performing team suffered an unintended consequence: blindly growing the head count broke the team's equilibrium.

A few months later, the senior director of the group hired a consultant to help fix the company's team formation issues. With this particular team, the consultant did only two things: they broke it into two teams and for both teams, established a clear purpose with metrics that defined progress toward their vision. Each team had its own Product Owner and a set of developer and test engineers. The functional manager became the cross-team.

One might think that having two teams would cause more coordination issues. However, if we remove the lens of big company thinking, then clear purpose and shared values dominate the need for ongoing alignment. A clear purpose keeps groups together during stressful times. Whenever a critical situation emerges inside a large company or even a team, purpose induces greater alignment.

Jeff Bezos is a big believer in small team formation because it allows decision making to be de-centralized and avoids the autocratic control of decisions. Many organizations where C-level executives end up making the lion's share of decisions suffer from a lack of diverse skillsets involved in the decision making.

Team formation also affords us the opportunity to scale hiring standards. A team should be empowered to hire in ways that fit the needs of the team and the cultural fabric the team chooses to promote. Think of this aspect in terms of *scaling teams* rather than *scaling headcount*.

Once again, let's take note: Amazon has shifted its approach and now measures the number of teams, instead of just headcount. How can you make this shift while working at a large company?

Regardless of existing company policy, Product Managers play a crucial role in defining a company's team formation. It is up to the Product Manager to organize the structure in such a way that a team is prepared to meet or beat certain business outcomes.

Let's say you report to a hierarchy, whether a Product Management hierarchy or an engineering hierarchy. You're ready to start a project with a clear set of desired outcomes. Now what?

For example, your team needs to achieve these goals:
1) Sensor reading and calibration as a function that provides response time outcomes accurate to one-millionth of a second from sensors to reduce latency delays

2) Mechanics settings functions that control all external mechanics for self-driving cars
3) And more

The first two goals are large domains and can be split up into smaller functions of seven to ten people each, as appropriate. For example, under the large domain of sensor reading and calibration, we may designate optical sensors as a separate team responsible for all optical sensors. Their vision would roll up into the domain's vision of a one-millionth-of-a-second response time from sensors. You may also consider introducing aggregator roles to ensure the cross-team experience is uniform. These roles are often known as group Product Managers or chief Product Owners.

Most engineering managers would likely build a great domain, but organizing that domain into clear-cut functions requires a deep, cultivated design acumen for Product Management.

This is perhaps the greatest unspoken value of awesome Product Management: *your team organization determines the overall quality and experience of your product or service.*

Folks like Steve Jobs organized departments, but they also defined functional units that provided clear value to their teams. Within organizations like Apple, team formation keeps the organization highly cohesive.

So, how do you know that your team needs to grow? The best tool a Product Manager has to get visibility on workload is a team's backlog, which represents the demand. Let's assume the demand is well-funded, and the team has to deliver to the commitments within a stipulated time frame. If the time is an important constraint, even in the startup world, the best recommendation is to slice the team. This isn't slicing the resources into two teams—instead, the Product Manager introduces a new backlog to hire and kick off a new team. The new team will then begin to define its own charter based on the master backlog and eventually create its own backlog. Uber has achieved explosive growth as an organization by not just by increasing developer headcount but also by creating full-staffed and functional teams. They hold the Product Owner accountable for growing and cloning a team as the workload grows. In lieu of adding a headcount to the team, they allow the team to organize their backlog to either grow or start another team.

COLLABORATION AND FLOW

Tight pods increase flow and collaboration among team members. When your team members don't have to shout across the room, you've reduced the friction in collaboration. On that note, how many people can you fit on a table?

Getting cozy reduces friction while improving collaboration and flow.

How do you hire? Or, how does your team hire? Hiring practices are *very* traditional, even today.

With so many social sites at our fingertips, it's easier to get visibility for available positions. On the other hand, the postings are overly standardized and fail to inform candidates applying for the job about the realities and nuance of the job, and vice versa, they hardly contain enough information to tell if the candidate is the right fit within the fabric of the company.

> *"Traditional interviews are all about two people sitting across from each other, lying to each other."*[51]
> — Rich Sheridan, CEO of Menlo Innovations

Menlo Innovations of Ann Arbor, Michigan, has perfected a collaborative approach to hiring, their work environment, and just about everything in between.

Instead of typical interviews, Menlo Innovations creates a series of unusual test situations in order to evaluate candidates. For a typical job opening, fifty candidates might come in together, then split up into pairs and work together on a specific task (often programming). Richard Sheridan, Menlo's CEO, often likes to give them another, rather unusual task: "Your job is to make the other person look good so that they get a second interview," he says.

Partners switch off, giving Menlo observers a chance to see how candidates handle a range of personalities and stresses. Simple behaviors, such as a raised voice or frustrated body language, are observed and noted. "It's like speed-dating," remarks Sheridan. Of those that try out, 40 percent are selected for the next round.

The second round is a paid day working side-by-side with Menlo employees. Roughly half of these candidates will be offered a paid three-week contract. If the trial period goes well, only then will they be offered the full-time job.

Once hired, employees participate in collaborative teams. The workspace is large and open, with long tables serving as desks. Employees are paired two per computer on each project and rotate every two weeks. While this might not be the ideal working environment for everyone, those for whom it is praise it highly.

Menlo's hiring process is designed to select for highly collaborative personalities. The company's employees are fundamentally teamwork oriented, so new hires are evaluated and gradually oriented to the company culture through the hiring process.

TEAM STRUCTURE

Spotify has an innovative, remarkably autonomous structure.[52] Eschewing traditional management hierarchies, the company divides workers into squads, tribes, chapters, and guilds.[53]

The basic unit of workers is called a squad. Each squad is responsible for a set of features or functions but maintains maximal autonomy. Because each squad is actually a full-stack team, it is responsible for handling both backend and user interface implementation across platforms. They're a bit like mini-startups.

Related squads are grouped into tribes—say, infrastructure or music player tribes.[54] The tribes behave as "incubators" for the startup-like squads. Tribes are capped at 100 people in order to keep them small and agile.

Tribes also act autonomously. When interaction is necessary, especially for specific projects, they communicate, but this is kept to a minimum. One major purpose of autonomy is to enable speed of execution. Quite literally, neither tribes nor squads should need to wait for outside approval or input.

A typical squad will include web service engineers, iOS, Android, web, and desktop engineers, as well as testers, an agile coach, a product owner, and an UX designer. The squad is built out and equipped to implement anything related to their feature.

Another key facet of Spotify's structure: squads don't have a single leader to whom everyone reports. Instead, the Product Owner and UX designer work collaboratively with all members of the team.

Spotify introduced groups, called guilds, that work across boundaries between squads and tribes. Membership in guilds is entirely voluntary, and they are self-organized around different technical or interest areas. For example, there are guilds for Web Development best practices, Agile Practices, Leadership, Test Automation, and so on.

Spotify's structure enables a remarkable level of organizational agility.[55] It is easy for the company to respond to market pressures immediately by creating new squads or dissolving old ones—without the messiness of changes to reporting structures. This flexibility-by-design avoids the pitfalls of traditional, hierarchal politics and positions the company for speed of execution.

SLOW DOWN, SO YOU CAN GO FASTER

In 2010, Waze had just closed a B-round of funding for $25 million and was expanding fast.[56] With a new level of resources at the ready, the team took a moment to reflect on how best to approach the next level of scaling.

As the Waze team looked through their rough data, they realized that while the number of users had been growing, the usage metrics themselves had stayed fairly flat.

In the rush to expand, the team had focused on adding users as their Most Important Thing (MIT). This single-minded focus had gotten them through a B round, but was it still the MIT?

At the time, Waze had less-than-optimal analytics capabilities. The company had poured its resources into engineering user features, instead of reporting and analysis. Noam Bardim, CEO of Waze, made the decision to halt all growth activities, step back, and analyze the situation. "We spent one month pulling reports, tagging new events, meeting with our users, and doing anything we could to better understand how Waze was being used," Bardim said.[57] "What we discovered was that our product was just not good enough, although the vision was."

The analysis showed that Waze had strong positioning and user acquisition, but the app itself was performing too poorly to retain users. With this insight, Waze reframed its MIT around a new metric: "90-day driver retention," or in other words, how many users who used the app to drive this month would still be driving with the app in ninety days. At the time, Waze had a meager 8 percent ninety days' driver retention in the US.

After this period of reorientation, Waze emerged with a newly defined a new MIT. To implement, they ceased hiring and funneled all efforts into achieving focused progress on the MIT. The team recorded an extensive list of product and feature issues—ranging from poor mapping to confusion over audio prompts—and got to work. "Six months later we hit 30 percent 90-day driver retention and it continued to grow from there," said Bardim. Three years later, Waze was acquired by Google for over a billion dollars.

At Waze, Product Management was credited with playing a key role by pausing, analyzing, defining, and reorienting to a new MIT.

Sometimes, to scale up fast, we have to slow down.

15 V2MOM—Vision, Values, Methods, Obstacles, Measures

> *"While a company is growing fast, there is nothing more important than constant communication and complete alignment."*[58]
>
> — Marc Benioff, Salesforce.com founder

As our teams grow, the North Star starts to get fuzzy. Inevitably, we begin to miss out on the WHY that should be animating our decisions and actions. There's just too much room for uncertainty, noise, competing interests, and all kinds of distraction—let alone entropy. *Why did we start down this path, and what's guiding us?*

Salesforce uses a unique tool called "V2MOM" to keep the organization aligned. Originally created by Mark Benioff, it is deployed at *every* level of the company, on every team, to this day.

V2MOM stands for *Vision, Values, Methods, Obstacles, Measures.* As you'll see in the following exercise, V2MOM is essentially a structured set of questions. It touches on each primary area with one question, from Vision to Measures.

The same set of questions can be put to use for complex goals, like acquiring companies, to smaller topics, like a discussion about a new product feature.

Though your organization might be using alternative goal frameworks, there's a lot to be learned from the simplicity of V2MOM. It's a proven way to define your vision, generate a roadmap, and keep your team aligned to a target as you work toward achieving it.

V2MOM EXERCISE
Think of a goal or a present-day challenge within your organization, then answer the following questions. You might have more than one answer, so be sure to prioritize.

Keep this exercise short—no longer than one page.

VISION: *What is your goal?*

_____

_____

VALUES: *What principles are necessary for achieving your vision and alignment during prioritization decisions?*

_____

_____

_____

METHODS: *What system(s) or means will you use?*

_____

_____

_____

OBSTACLES: *How might progress be blocked?*

_____

_____

_____

MEASURES: *How will you know you got there?*

_____

_____

_____

A V2MOM is a living document. It can be redone at intervals or span many years, depending on your needs. It helps define your goals and the roadmap to achieving them, while allowing for creative evolution.

As a catalyst, this simple document has the power to bring members of the organization into alignment around a vision. "V2MOM is the glue that binds us together," says Marc Benioff.[59]

Imagine you're the Product Manager for ecommerce site check-out team . . . how would you compose your V2MOM?

Going further, how would you work with your team to build a V2MOM and keep it alive throughout the year?

16 How to Challenge Your Team to Learn Continuously

> *"I used to think that to make something happen in a corporation or in the army, you had to be at the higher ranks, to be a general. But you just need to start a movement."*
>
> — Tom Kelley, Creative Confidence:
> Unleashing the Creative Potential Within Us All

Many leaders seek to prove themselves, but resort to commanding and controlling as a methodology for getting work done. These leaders use fear as a motivation—but this shortsighted tactic simply doesn't work beyond the short term.

The topic of leadership is particularly important for Product Managers:

- *How can we influence our teams to be on a learning journey?*
- *How can we provide air cover and safety for our teams as we allow them space to form and grow?*

Carol Dweck created the concept of a "growth" mindset—in other words, a belief in oneself as able to learn and grow. In her research, Dweck found that nurses in a hospital who were able to talk freely about mistakes (so others could learn and improve) made fewer mistakes than those in hospitals where supervisors ruled by fear. Dweck also found that in coercive situations, people quickly figure out how to game the system.

Today's management is change management. No one escapes change, and almost all challenges are adaptive in nature. Each scenario we face is complex, and our brains naturally and inescapably perceive the uncertainty as a threat.

How do we as Product Managers use a growth mindset to make change more manageable?

Teams perceive change as either:
- **Fear**—as a negative emotion, fear causes distress and reduces performance.
- **Challenge**—a challenge can produce stress, but it also creates a positive catalyst. It can prompt the team to come together, rally, and become more energized.

Teams cling to the way things are, and they perceive just about any change as a threat. If we want to avoid uncertainty converting to fear, we might ask: *How do we challenge a team just enough to energize them, so it doesn't transfer into fear?*

However, such a question is itself framed negatively, as it focuses on "avoiding" a negative outcome.

There are many more enlightening and potentially powerful questions to ask instead:
- *How do you channel the emotions of your team?*
- *How can you use emotion as fuel for engagement on your team?*
- *How can they lean on each other?*

We've seen teams build new skills like Google Home Voice interactions using Google's APIs on the first day they were hired. Applying creative muscle to new technologies while still learning and developing a skillset is an amazing opportunity.

From creating an experience on Google Assistant to programming automatic braking for driverless cars, every aspect of creating a product requires a great deal of creativity. Our capacity to grow is foundationally dependent on our ability to "fail" and learn quickly.

When we walk around thinking we have a certain ability with an existing skill set and we don't need to learn anything new, we're stuck in a fixed mindset. We compare ourselves with other people as a primary means of getting better. If a team thinks they want to do mobile only because of an XYZ reason, that isn't a growth mindset.

If you're operating in a growth mindset, you're focused on getting smarter simply because you want to, even if you don't have a means to demonstrate your knowledge. You are focused on your progress over time and believe that improvement is possible.

You might think to yourself, "I'm not a geek or coding person." But this needn't be the end of the story. We can reframe the thought positively and empower growth by asking, "How can I learn one thing, right now? How can I write one line of HTML code and really understand it?" *A growth mindset is oriented toward learning.*

This doesn't mean you're never going to be frustrated. If a team picks up a book and sets up a learning schedule, that's a growth mindset team. They don't question poor skills or fear making mistakes, because they know they'll learn to meet the challenge. They're able to work through the less-than-optimal bits and stumble across the barriers on the way to becoming a better-learning team.

As we mentioned in Chapter 14, employees at Menlo innovation work in pairs. Sometimes, pairs need to pick up new technical skills to finish work for a given sprint, but they don't move work off to another team that's super skilled in that particular technology. Instead, they put their growth mindset to work and learn from each other as they go forward.

When you encounter a tough patch and need to ramp up an uncomfortable skillset, try thinking, "I may not have done as well as I wanted to, but I've given my best and I continue to get better."

Sometimes, you'll see your team oscillate between two states. *How can you make your team spend more time in growth mindset thinking?*

You can't *force* a team to adopt a growth mindset, but you can grease the wheels and increase the chances.

To test your process, try setting up a learning lab—but keep in mind that how you go about this test will determine its outcome. The same sprint can be carried out according to a fixed mindset or a growth mindset, depending on the outlook. If a team feels the sprint is a measure of how much work they get done, they're in fixed mindset thinking. If the same team has the goal of maximizing learning during the sprint and signs up for a number of experiments to carry it out, they're much more oriented toward a growth mindset.

Teams operating with a growth mindset do their best work in challenging situations. They welcome the opportunity to dig in and lean on each other to make things happen, they're not worried about failure, and they're able to absorb negative feedback as a gift.

This doesn't mean that all emotions will be positive. Team members will still encounter moments of feeling bad—what's important is how they choose to react to those feelings. If you succumb to a negative impact, you're in a fixed mindset. If the same situation is fuel for engagement and prompts you to overcome a challenge, then you're making strong steps toward a growth mindset.

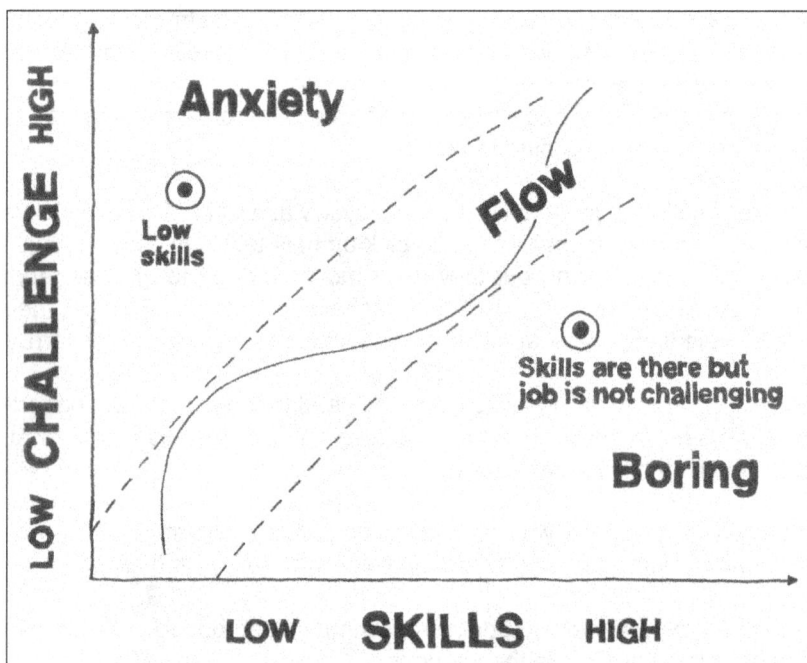

A leader needs to keep their team within a "sweet spot"—there should be just enough tension to tip them into the productive range and a flow state.

But if a leader can't regulate tension and it spikes, it's almost certain that the team's performance will go from a peak to a sharp drop, with subsequent work avoidance.

Chapter 16: How to Challenge Your Team to Learn Continuously

Emotional skills are a superpower—they enable us to better manage our team's mindset and emotional environment.

Emotional skills for leadership:
- Have faith in your own ability to continue to develop through learning.
- Have faith in your team's ability to learn and your goal to help them develop.
- Cultivate a strong belief in teamwork.
- Provide your team with a sense of psychological safety by helping them feel safe and able to grow.

We recommend de-scaling a desired behavior to one or two people at first, and then growing it from there.

Like any change in habits, *start very small*. Imagine building the habit of working out as soon as you wake up. Initially, it might be too challenging to do a full workout. Deconstructing your goal—for example, after waking up, do a simple sixty-second routine—will improve your chances of creating a continued behavior. You could break down the proposed habit even further and begin with the goal of completing just one pushup after waking up.

Watch out for the internal monologue of a fixed mindset. You might observe thoughts like, *I'm not good at this*, *I don't think I can*, or *It's not easy for me*. These thoughts are obstacles to productive action, and with attention and persistence, you can rewrite these thought patterns as new, productive, growth mindset habits.

In the spirit of starting small, work with your team to design short, quick experimental actions that will engage the group in a growth mindset.

Growth mindset team experiments:
- Design time for you and your team to actively plan in a new learning area. Time to play and learn prepares the foundation for inspiration later on.
- Share stories about what you've learned. Storytelling builds rapport and communicates a more complete picture than mere bullet points.
- Host brown bags to share both awesome demos moments, as well as mistakes and vulnerabilities. Honesty and vulnerability build connection and increase a team's capacity to respond to challenges.

- After a retrospective, pair up and carve out short time frames to roll out change experiments.

Remember, *you are the key to changing your team.* To lead others, you must first start by embracing change yourself.

If you can apply growth mindset to yourself, you'll undoubtedly learn more about your team and will be primed to design small experiments to support their change journey.

HOW TO BECOME A PM

17 What Is a Product Owner?

> "Everybody loves a hero. People line up for them, cheer them, and scream their names. And years later, they'll tell how they stood in the rain for hours just to get a glimpse of the one who taught them how to hold on a second longer."
>
> — May Parker, Spider Man 2

Job titles in our subject area are frequently debated by enterprises large and small. You might wonder, and it's important to clarify: *What is a Product Owner? Why don't we call them Product Managers?* Different teams answer this question in different ways.

Generally, for smaller teams, these roles are played by the same person. Organizations refer to this as PO = PM, where PM is the Product Manager from the job function of Product Management.

Not all Product Owners have to be from Product Management. For example, on technical teams, we might find that the right person to play Product Owner comes from engineering.

The word Product Owner emerged from the Scrum Framework. So, if your organization uses Scrum, there's a high likelihood you'll hear both PO and PM. Simply put, PO is the role on the team, and PM is the title. It isn't necessary that the PO on your team will be from Product Management.

In short, let your organization design owners help you figure out the role and the responsibilities, and then choose the most fitting role name. Many companies are moving to newer role names for this function. For example, Menlo Innovations calls these employees, "High Tech Anthropologists," because their organization design is focused on customer-centric problems and need identification. Companies may choose to combine elements of UX and Product Management to produce a hybrid role under Product Management. There's no set standard and outcomes depend on the organization's context.

Before we dive into details, let's look at the role of a business analyst. Some organizations confuse this role with Product Management, as BAs share certain responsibilities, i.e., they develop requirements and test software developed by the team.

While BAs may be good candidates for Product Management, we often ignore that Product Management has a far greater level of responsibility and requires a more expansive mindset. In a few scenarios—like one-to-one platform migration or platform upgrades—BAs play a critical role and are more suited to the job than a Product Manager.

A rule of thumb: *when the path is known and the tactical nature of the work is more critical, a BA may be better suited for the project.*

Key Responsibilities of a Product Owner
Tracks the overall market and competitive landscape
Manages the long-term roadmap, involving stakeholders from various groups; the ideas are expressed as epics
Supports other non-technical organizations (such as sales, marketing, and channel)
Writes epics and stories/requirements
Attends Scrum meetings, including standups, retrospectives, and demos
Leads backlog grooming to decompose/estimate stories
Creates mockups and works with UX on design
Answers questions from developers, clarifies requirements, etc.
Documents the new feature for implementations and release notes

Writes acceptance criteria
Demonstrates latest iteration to stakeholders outside of the team (pre-release) and gathers feedback

This role is one of the most important to enable the vision and focus for a team. Depending on the capacity needed, you may split the responsibilities for one or two people.

As a general good practice, we recommend that each team have one Product Owner who owns prioritization of the backlog. They may interact with multiple stakeholders to build the backlog.

Before you implement, beware—*many companies try to wing folks into this role without the right training and guidance.*

Some leading product companies have established Product Owner boot camps. They start with three to four days of immersive core product skills training, including: getting out into the field with real questions for real customers, attending calls at customer care, being part of hackathons, creating personas, and participating in active Lean coffee community forums.

Here's a quick way to identify whether a company has a tightly-knit product owner community: simply visit their home page on a desktop, and then on mobile. If you see a disjointed experience, you can tell that the silos don't talk to each other. Even simple cues—like the check-out experience differing from a product view page—speak volumes about how an organization sets up (or doesn't) these roles for success.

One large enterprise (the travel industry) solves the problem of organizational silos using a different type of team formation. Rather than having separate Product Owners for their iOS team, Android team, and web development team, they choose to have only a single product owner across a slice of platform.

The "slice" product owner focuses on the type of problem they're working on and resolves it across all platforms. This approach provides a tremendous amount of appropriate experience parity (not feature parity) and avoids the tendency of functional teams to trap thinking in silos.

In addition, the company maintains a truly cross-functional cross-platform team that cuts across all slices of the platform. Structural changes like these have technical debt implications and should be carefully designed.

Many companies have the following key requirements in job descriptions for the Product Owner role:

What you'll do

- *Drive the high-level vision for this product area.*
- *Lead research and engineering efforts to produce new metrics and models.*
- *Interface with teams across the company to integrate outputs into various initiatives.*
- *Set up a learnings/feedback cycle to integrate results from experimentation into the work of the team.*

Beyond distinctions and labels, the heart of the role is the inspiring vision a team creates together. *The success of the Product Manager or Product Owner depends on the value they create for their end customer via team empowerment.* In our experience, less than 10 percent of Product Owners are really successful at doing this.

We believe that every team needs an awesome Product Owner on board to help the team realize its full potential. The Product Owner should be data driven toward features they choose to work on, fearless at saying NO, and relentless about their focus on outcomes.

In a multi-team scenario, they have an important additional responsibility: *Product Owners should talk to each other.*

We should organize teams and backlogs to minimize dependencies, but there will always be some dependencies. Product Owners should maintain synchronization, so the organization can build things in a sensible order and avoid sub-optimization. In large projects, this usually calls for a Chief Product Owner role to keep the Product Owners synchronized.

18 How Do You Become a Product Owner?

"At the end of the day, your job is to minimize output, and maximize outcome and impact."

— Jeff Patton, User Story Mapping: Discover the Whole Story, Build the Right Product

---

You might be approaching this question from one of many possible fields—perhaps you're an Engineer, BA, Software tech worker, or entrepreneur—or you might have any type of background where you built products.

No matter your background, in order to step into the role of a Product Owner, you'll need exposure to many new aspects of product creation. In this chapter, we're going to stretch your cross-functional skills and expand your comfort zone.

> **Question:** *How do you become a Product Owner?*[60]
> **Simple answer:** *Learning by doing work within the context of your industry.*

Let's start by addressing a few basics: if I'm a developer, can I be a Product Manager? Well, it depends on the context.

For technology products, some developers may turn out to be more awesome Product Managers than non-developers. What enables them to make the crossover—is it experience, skill set, or a relentless focus on customer needs and outcomes?

We've often seen Product Owners (interchange: Product Managers) learn more about their customers by diving in and becoming customers themselves. One Product Owner we knew wore a black band over her eyes for two hours every day. It helped her experience firsthand how blind people used her company's product, in this case, extensions in a smartphone. It's up to each Product Owner to educate, experiment, and get to know their customers and their needs.

Some years ago, we met Emma, a Product Manager working with a large retailer to launch a pharmacy application (her name has been changed for privacy). She wasn't the first Product Manager—her team had seen two previous Product Managers come and go before she joined, and both had left the team within a few months. So, what made Emma stick, and how did she succeed with this team where others had failed?

Emma was new to pharmacy and mobile as a domain. However, she compensated by having an open and learning-oriented mindset. She spent hours in the field doing research at local CVS or Walgreens stores. She talked to consumers and asked them open questions: Why did they chose this particular location, and how happy were they? Would they recommend the pharmacy to their family or friends?

Emma went on these field walks with one or two members of her team and made copious amounts of notes. She wanted to both define and understand the different sets of customers who entered the pharmacy. She also talked to pharmacists while they were on their lunch break, looking to learn more about their experiences. She even spent time talking to local doctors who referred patients to these nearby pharmacies.

Based on her interviews, she developed multiple consumer profiles (or personas) and started to layer their needs. She did this every day with a few members of her team, and gradually a vision and strategy for the mobile app began to form. Within two months, the app launched with four main features: prescription reorder, prescription rewards, track order status, and reminders that could be manually set.

Within a few days of the launch, this app became the most downloaded app in the retail pharmaceutical business. Emma was able to defy all traditional norms of Product Management and didn't focus her core efforts in writing user stories or creating backlogs. She spent a tremendous amount of time on defining the right set of problems and then thin slicing the learnings into multiple versions of her release. Similar apps were released for iPad, targeting moms with younger kids. Reminders for flu shots and auto-update features for various administrative tasks made these releases very successful.

Emma gained a tremendous amount of confidence in the mobile field. She joined meetup groups and followed thought leaders in this space. She found a mentor within the company who helped her grow, and she learned from her mentor's experience of launching a mobile grocery app in an international market. She developed a dynamic support system and constantly collaborated on ideas and information.

A few years later, Emma left to form her own consulting company around mobile app development. She continues to learn by hiring up-and-coming folks within this space. When we asked her how this helps her career growth, she answered, "The newbies keep me fresh and on my toes. Since they're looking at things from a beginner's mindset, it helps me be more honest and keeps my learning journey going."

We asked Emma how she stays up to date on the world of Product Management. Here are her favorite five sources:

1) **Products That Count**—a meetup group in downtown San Francisco organized by S.C. Moatti, a mobile thought leader and the author of *Mobilized*

2) **Lean Product & Lean UX Silicon Valley**—a meetup in Palo Alto, California, run by Product Management and Lean Startup thought leader Dan Olsen, the author of *The Lean Product Playbook*

3) **Selected news**—news from groups like IDEO and Stanford Business School.

4) **Lean Startup Conference**—making time to go to the Lean Startup conference every year

5) **Quarterly learning goals**—setting quarterly goals to learn more about one topic; currently, she is learning about the Internet of Things and follows multiple leaders on YouTube and Twitter to stay up to date

Emma has taken multiple Product Management courses as part of her professional development; however, she didn't start with any one course in particular. There are too many options available, and most successful Product Owners are developed on the job.

Even though she isn't looking for a job, Emma does multiple interviews per quarter. The conversations in these job interviews drive her to think beyond her usual norms.

Her motto is to learn from failures, whether her own or those of others. She genuinely strives to make her clients and teams successful, and these values show in her work every day. She talks less process and maintains a laser focus on creating better outcomes. Her gutsiness makes her a great Product Manager.

Now, let's get know Julie (her name has also been changed), an intern at a large technology company invested in making self-driving software. In her new role, she's learning core skills like robotics control software. Her background in statistics and probability got her noticed for the position and will be critical for the job. Some of the skills she'll need weren't part of her university curriculum, but a year with the startup will help her get up to speed in machine learning, infrared sensitive radars, etc.

What if Julie wanted to prepare for a job as a Product Manager, so she could roll out a self-driving taxi fleet service? She'd need a different set of skills in addition to the above. Where she should go to start gaining this knowledge would depend on her exposure to different industries. Generally, people would opt for this role within an industry they've worked for.

Julie might consider gaining skills with government regulations and consider internationalization in the context of self-driving cars. LinkedIn resources are very helpful for emerging fields—e.g., self-driving groups on LinkedIn. Don't forget fieldwork (which might even be fun on occasion): Julie could test-drive a Tesla to experience how the company is shifting toward autonomous driving.

Many companies have a job family for Product Management. As a starting point, we suggest that all aspiring Product Managers look at jobs within their company and do a gap analysis of the core skills they bring to the table and existing gaps.

The best way to address gaps is to do real work, not just classroom trainings. Classroom teaching can provide an overview, but it doesn't expose you to actual industry scenarios. For example, in a classroom, you might learn about retail PO, but such learning can't be implemented back on your job in financial services.

The best Product Owners are built with on-the-job training. Good learners do activities like peer lunches as a way to get to know what their peers are working on.

If you make a plan for each of your gaps and begin to execute on your learning journey, you'll be well on your way to landing your next job.

Just start!

19 Negotiating and Listening

> *"Deep listening is the kind of listening that can help relieve the suffering of another person. You can call it compassionate listening. You listen with only one purpose: to help him or her to empty his heart."*[61]

— Thích Nhất Hạnh, Spiritual Leader

On the surface, listening might seem like a passive, almost submissive state. However, if you take the time to really practice, you'll notice that it takes a lot of energy and attention . . . *because true listening is a very active, very powerful state.*

Earlier in the book, we talked about listening in the context of orienting toward your customer and defining their needs as you develop a product vision—yet there's much more to listening.

Product Management involves constant negotiation with your team, stakeholders, and management, and the first step to negotiation is deep, active listening. Listening is the first and most primary factor in connecting with your team, customer, negotiation partner, and anyone else.

Pause, look around, find a human connection, and you'll go faster.

You don't listen when you're tired, and sure enough, your team stops listening when they're tired. If a team tells you they're right, it implies that they get it and they're listening. But if a team says you're right, it's more likely that they're asking you to move out of their way.

Being told what won't work is a better way to get your team to align with your vision.

Focus on building relationships at every opportunity. Relationship building is a long-term, profitable investment.

> **Question:** *How do you negotiate a deadline?*
> **Answer:** *Ask questions to regulate the tension.*
> - Could you tell me what's wrong with this?
> - How do we get everyone to align?
> - How do we know things are going to be on track?
> - What do we do if we know things aren't on track?
> - Could you help me identify the longer-term levers here?

You're not going to buy the drug because it is profitable, but because it is safe and very effective for your patients. Start with why they'll say no. Help them arrive at why they'll say no, but since you're not there, it will cause them to throw a better deal for you.

Let's take a situation where you, as a Product Manager, have immense pressure to get the team to prioritize a certain feature that's good for the customer. However, the tech lead on the team insists that the team spend the next two sprints (roughly four weeks) to work on tech debt and build additional monitoring for the application. The tech lead is tired and concerned: for the last six months, the team has been building new features with almost no time to refactor. How do you negotiate in this situation?

First, start with the capacity and the currency you naturally possess. Are you able to delay the planning meeting until you can sort this out? Or, do you need this now and you're pretty much in a bind if you don't start immediately?

Here are a few possible outcomes:
- Scenario A: You win, but the tech lead has something to hope for.
- Scenario B: You win something and he wins something.
- Scenario C: He loses and gets out of your way.
- Scenario D: *Avoid thinking about these scenarios and focus on your listening.*

Always open with understanding and empathy for the tech lead's position. You might say, "I think it's awesome we're starting to focus on this tech debt that's been building up. We waste a great deal of time debugging and fixing issues."

Next, pause, stay gentle, and *keep listening*. Don't jump in by taking the side of the business. Carefully listen to the tech lead's complete articulation of the problem. If you speak in any way, it should only be to help them express why this tech debt is crucial for the success of the team. You should hear out their view completely, until everything has been said and their chest is clear.

Once they have finished pouring their heart out, a window of opportunity will be offered to you, either through circumstances or directly. The window may be as simple as the tech lead asking you, "So, why does Kate need this now? What is the issue?" Or it may be simple as, "I'm sorry, I wish I could help you."

When this happens, you must resist every temptation to give in and explain how you need their help. Instead, continue to listen and surprise them by asking, "How can I help you get this prioritized? What can I do to get that developer request pushed through?" Or, "Can we spend the next three days meeting less, so the developers can simply focus on their work?" *Ask them how you can help them.*

At this point, just about every technical lead will move into your corner and start to say, "We'll get this done, but let's see what we can do get the new feature moving forward!"

Maybe the scene doesn't go the way you'd like—*you still need to stay calm and continue to listen.* Even if the situation doesn't change immediately, you will benefit immensely from this approach. It will enable you to build lifelong relationships, and the problem will no longer be yours alone.

Let's imagine you're dealing with an alpha personality who feels the need to win at all costs. You should identify that character trait and learn how to pace them. They should never feel a lack of control. When you want to slow someone like this down, ask a powerful question: "How can we do that now and keep our business partners happy? I really want to know how I can support you in helping our team." The alpha personality should feel respected at all times. They need to feel that they're very important. Stroke their ego by saying, "Our whole team, including me, is fully behind you and this idea. This is definitely key! You're helping us be awesome!"

When you next encounter an alpha personality,
identify their character trait and learn how to pace them.
Photo by Carlos Cram on Unsplash

Another powerful technique to get more information is to say something not fully correct, and thereby give power to the other person to correct you. Most people love to correct other people, it's an involuntary response. Once they correct you, it provides an automatic pathway to develop further inroads into the conversation. This natural process of correction will help ensure that your team members feel understood— it's an excellent technique for pacing discussions.

Your success is tied to your ability to master emotional stress. Find out what makes your leader and your team tick. This will be your leverage during times of influence and negotiation.

Constantly look for opportunities and be ready. It helps when you're able to relate to an ask by your technical lead, as you know that it sounds like that other brilliant idea the team implemented five sprints ago, and you saved two days every sprint just by doing it: "I love it! How do we do that? Initially, the business didn't agree to that either, but we worked through it." That's when they know you get their pain and you enter their circle of trust. You have to use their path and make it yours!

When your team believes in you, you'll have a greater ability to influence each situation.

One last but nearly always overlooked way to influence your team is to *be their biggest spokesperson*. Your team needs to be seen and appreciated. Spreading appreciation through your words and actions is magnetic and will help bind your team together through thick and thin.

Conclusion

Product Management in each of the scenarios we've discussed—whether Uber, Zipcar, SAP, Spotify, or any one of the world's most successful companies—follows a basic pattern of values:

> **Vision:** A clear need identified for the customers
> **Strategy:** A simple but powerful strategy
> **Rapid learning:** Fast experimentation
> **Team:** A group that perseveres every day to get closer to the vision

In this rapidly changing world where artificial intelligence will be making many decisions, Product Managers need to get even closer to customer insights. Without a rigorous, laser focus on customer needs, the chance of building an irrelevant product increases exponentially.

This book isn't just about the practices that support Product Management. In addition to skills, we've given you a framework for understanding the "building blocks" of true breakthroughs in Product Management.

In a recent shareholders letter, Jeff Bezos wrote about living as if every day at Amazon is still Day 1. "I've been reminding people that it's Day 1 for a couple of decades. . . . Day 2 is stasis. Followed by irrelevance. Followed by excruciating, painful decline. Followed by death."

The framework we've provided—vision, strategy, rapid learning, and team—will orient you toward the dawn of your own, ongoing Day 1.

What will your product takeoff be?

Approach the following questions as an opportunity to engage a growth mindset. By working out answers to these questions, you'll be defining a 360-degree understanding of Product Ownership and Management and preparing yourself for success in today's environment.

When you're finished or even as you work, share your answers with peers to stimulate discussion and grow your team-building skills.

1) What is innovation?
2) Why do we need Product Management?
3) How can we learn quickly on large platform migrations or products? Or, how does PM apply to platform products?
4) Give an example of how being bold is relevant to you.
5) What is a Product Owner? Why don't we call them Product Managers?
6) How do you become a Product Owner?
7) Is the Product Owner the CEO of the Product? Considering Amazon Music as an example, what does this mean?
8) What's the difference between a Business Analyst and Product Owner?
9) Who should be the Product Owner?
10) Who should be the Product Owner for a Platform team?
11) I'm not technical enough. Can I still be a Product Owner?
12) What is continuous delivery, and what do I need to do to implement it?

13) What are the success measures for your role?

14) What are the success measures for your Product Management function?

15) How is Product Management different for web product and a mobile app?

16) How do you hire great Product Owners?

17) How do you kill products or end the lives of products?

18) If you acquire a new product, is it an innovation? For example, Microsoft acquired LinkedIn. What is their product strategy?

19) Regarding change management around Product Management, do you think Product Managers are also change agents?

20) How can a change of ecosystems focus our innovation efforts? Use investing in mobile-first strategy over enormous web development efforts as an example.

21) Discuss the new age of voice recognition products: Alexa, Google, and Deep Speech 2.

22) What is machine learning? How will you incorporate its foundational principles into the products you build?

23) Are customer acquisition channels that are non-electronic valid? Why are bookstores bouncing back?

24) Explain the five tactical things every Product Manager should know: vision boards and success metrics, roadmaps, release planning, breaking down work, and prioritizing work.

25) Define a bold vision based on your work to date.

26) How is Product Management different in a startup compared to an enterprise?

27) *What is one thing you've learned from this book that you'll try now?*

Endnotes

1 "Walt Disney's Carousel of Progress," Walt Disney World Resort (website), Disney, https://disneyworld.disney.go.com/attractions/magic-kingdom/walt-disney-carousel-of-progress/.

2 "Walt Disney's Carousel of Progress," Wikipedia, Wikimedia Foundation, last modified May 7, 2018, 14:15, https://en.wikipedia.org/wiki/Walt_Disney%27s_Carousel_of_Progress.

3 Lia Ryerson, "There's a ride at Disney that will never shut down, no matter what — here's why," February 21, 2018, 2:27 p.m., http://www.thisisinsider.com/disneys-carousel-of-progress-will-never-close-2018-2.

4 Dave Smith, "Krystina, Avondale, Arizona," D23: The Official Disney Fan Club, Disney, https://d23.com/ask-dave/krystina-avondale-arizona-2/. This quote is frequently misattributed to Walt Disney. As noted by the Disney Archives, it was actually written by Imagineer Tom Fitzgerald for the Horizons attraction at Epcot.

5 Owen Thomas, "Apple: Hello, iPhone," CNN Money, Cable News Network, January 9, 2007, 5:36 p.m., http://money.cnn.com/2007/01/09/technology/apple_jobs/.

6 "The Mercedes-Benz F 015 Luxury in Motion," Mercedes-Benz, Daimler, https://www.mercedes-benz.com/en/mercedes-benz/innovation/research-vehicle-f-015-luxury-in-motion/.

7 David Undercoffler, "CES 2015: Mercedes-Benz shows off self-driving car of the future," *Los Angeles Times*, Los Angeles Times, January 5, 2015, 10:58 p.m., http://www.latimes.com/business/autos/la-fi-hy-ces-2015-mercedes-autonomous-20150105-story.html.

8 Emily Roberts, "Introducing the Amazon Dash Button and Dash Replenishment Service," Appstore Blogs, Amazon.com, Inc., March 21, 2015, https://developer.amazon.com/blogs/appstore/

post/Tx3N3VXXO52B15I/introducing-the-amazon-dash-button-and-dash-replenishment-service.

9 James Surowiecki, "Where Nokia Went Wrong," *The New Yorker*, Condé Nast, updated September 3, 2013, http://www.newyorker.com/business/currency/where-nokia-went-wrong.

10 "Taxicabs of the United States," Wikipedia, Wikimedia Foundation, last modified June 14, 2018, 08:34, https://en.wikipedia.org/wiki/Taxicabs_of_the_United_States

11 "Oprah Talks to Thich Nhat Hanh," Oprah.com, Harpo, Inc., http://www.oprah.com/spirit/oprah-talks-to-thich-nhat-hanh.

12 Ibid., page 5.

13 Justin Bariso, "Elon Musk Takes Customer Complaint on Twitter From Idea to Execution in 6 Days," *Inc.*, Manuseto Ventures, https://www.inc.com/justin-bariso/elon-musk-takes-customer-complaint-on-twitter-from-idea-to-execution-in-6-days.html.

14 Ibid.

15 "Joichi Ito quote," AZ Quotes, AZQuotes.com, http://www.azquotes.com/quote/731979.

16 "Number of monthly active Facebook users worldwide as of 1st quarter 2018 (in millions)," Statista, Statista Inc., https://www.statista.com/statistics/264810/number-of-monthly-active-facebook-users-worldwide/.

17 Chris Pruett, "LinkedIn Desktop Redesign Puts Conversations and Content at the Center," Official LinkedIn Blog, LinkedIn Corporation, January 19, 2017, https://blog.linkedin.com/2017/january/19/linkedin-desktop-redesign-puts-conversations-and-content-at-the-center.

18 Sharky Liu, "What is Dropbox? Explained! Original Dropbox Video [HD]," YouTube video, 2:17, June 14, 2012, https://www.youtube.com/watch?v=xy9nSnalvPc.

19 "Apple Developer Program," Apple Developer, Apple Inc., https://developer.apple.com/programs/.

20 Christopher Lawton, "Inside SAP's Skunkworks as It Takes Aim at Oracle," *The Wall Street Journal,* Dow Jones & Company Inc., January 26, 2012, https://www.wsj.com/articles/SB10001424052970203430404577092651330963684.

21 Ibid.

22 "Home Page," Safecast, Momoko Ito Foundation, https://blog.safecast.org/.

23 Micah Solomon, "How To Think Like Apple About The Customer Service Experience," *Forbes*, Forbes Media LLC, November 21, 1013, 4:58 p.m., https://www.forbes.com/sites/micahsolomon/2014/11/21/how-apple-thinks-differently-about-the-customer-service-experience-and-how-it-can-help-you/#15d77bc627c9.

24 Elon Musk, Twitter post, December 17, 2016, 5:05 a.m., https://twitter.com/elonmusk/status/810108760010043392?lang=en.

25 "Quotes in Statistics & Science," Department of Statistics, The Board of Regents of the University of Wisconsin, https://www.stat.wisc.edu/quotes.

26 "Successful LEGO Strategy Delivers Continued Strong Growth," About Us LEGO.com, The LEGO Group, February 21, 2013, https://www.lego.com/en-us/aboutus/news-room/2013/february/annual-result-2012.

27 Richard Sheridan, Twitter post, March 22, 2015, 6:02 a.m., https://twitter.com/menloprez/status/579629235720994816.

28 "How Design Thinking Transformed Airbnb from a Failing Startup to a Billion Dollar Business," First Round Review, First Round, http://firstround.com/review/How-design-thinking-transformed-Airbnb-from-failing-startup-to-billion-dollar-business/.

29 Ibid.

30 Avery Hartmans, "How the career of Ryan Graves, Uber's first billionaire CEO, was launched by a single tweet," *Business Insider*, Insider Inc., August 10, 2017, 2:59 p.m., http://www.businessinsider.com/ryan-graves-uber-tweet-career-2017-8.

31 "Google X Head On Moonshots: 10x Is Easier Than 10 Percent," *Wired*, Condé Nast, February 11, 2013, 06:30 a.m., https://www.wired.com/2013/02/moonshots-matter-heres-how-to-make-them-happen/.

32 Jeremy Quittner, "Robin Chase: How I Survived a Huge Screw-up," *Inc.*, Manuseto Ventures, February 28, 2013, http://www.inc.com/magazine/201303/how-i-got-started/robin-chase.html.

33 Erin Griffith, "Jack Dorsey's Vision for Twitter Becomes Clear," *Fortune*, Time Inc., February 11, 2016, http://fortune.com/2016/02/10/jack-dorseys-vision-for-twitter-becomes-clear/

34 Sean Hollister, "Sorry, Snapchat: The glassholes are coming," CNET, CBS Interactive Inc., November 19, 2016, 5:00 a.m., https://www.cnet.com/news/snapchat-spectacles-glassholes-google-glass/.

35 "About Us," GoPro, GoPro, Inc., https://gopro.com/about-us.

36 "Quote by Helen Keller," Goodreads, Goodreads Inc., https://www.goodreads.com/quotes/9411-alone-we-can-do-so-little-together-we-can-do.

37 One of the best resources in the industry for Product Managers is the Innovation Games, a high-collaboration platform. To learn more about Innovation games, visit: https://weave.conteneo.co/a/innovationgames/1.

38 As an exercise, please visit https://squareup.com/reader and parse the page into different front, back, and bottom combinations on a cereal box.

39 Chris Hadfield, "Chris Hadfield: Earth-bound," Macleans.ca, Rogers Media, October 23, 2013, http://www.macleans.ca/culture/earth-bound/.

40 "Slack's Founder On How They Became a $1 Billion Company In Two Years," Fast Company, Fast Company & Inc., February 4, 2015, https://www.fastcompany.com/3041905/slacks-founder-on-how-they-became-a-1-billion-company-in-two-years.

41 Tren Griffin, "12 Things about Product-Market Fit," *Andreessen Horowitz*, Andreessen Horowitz, February 18, 2017, http://a16z.com/2017/02/18/12-things-about-product-market-fit/.

42 Ibid.

43 Ibid.

44 "From 0 to $1B - Slack's Founder Shares Their Epic Launch Strategy," First Round Review, First Round, http://firstround.com/review/From-0-to-1B-Slacks-Founder-Shares-Their-Epic-Launch-Strategy/.

45 "Slack's Founder On How They Became a $1 Billion Company In Two Years," Fast Company, Fast Company & Inc., February 4, 2015, https://www.fastcompany.com/3041905/slacks-founder-on-how-they-became-a-1-billion-company-in-two-years.

46 "From 0 to $1B - Slack's Founder Shares Their Epic Launch Strategy," First Round Review, First Round, http://firstround.com/review/From-0-to-1B-Slacks-Founder-Shares-Their-Epic-Launch-Strategy/.

47 Janko Roettgers, "Roku Got Close to $400 Million Revenue in 2016," *Variety*, Variety Media, LLC, February 28, 2017, 6:00 a.m., http://variety.com/2017/digital/news/roku-2016-revenue-1201998433/

48 Pushpa Makhija, "How to Use Cohort Analysis to Improve Customer Retention," CleverTap, WizRocket, Inc., March 28, 2016, https://clevertap.com/blog/how-to-use-cohort-analysis-to-improve-customer-retention/

49 Victor Lipman, "Phil Jackson Brings NY Knicks 'Mindful' Management," *Forbes*, Forbes Media LLC, October 15, 2014, 01:01 p.m., https://www.forbes.com/sites/victorlipman/2014/10/15/phil-jackson-brings-ny-knicks-mindful-management/.

50 JIRA is an agile project tracking tools used by agile teams. Visit https://www.atlassian.com/software/jira.

51 Donna Fein, "The Weirdest Interview Advice You'll Ever Get: Don't Ask Questions," CBS News, CBS Interactive Inc., last updated November 9, 2010, 5:04 p.m., https://www.cbsnews.com/news/the-weirdest-interview-advice-youll-ever-get-dont-ask-questions/.

52 Watch Spotify Engineering Culture, Part 1: https://www.youtube.com/watch?v=Mpsn3WaI_4k&list=PLC3mk_XNnmVS7HG_nhNr3I1VQ-2eL2XgB.

53 Watch Spotify Engineering Culture, Part 2: https://www.youtube.com/watch?v=X3rGdmoTjDc&list=PLC3mk_XNnmVS7HG_nhNr3l1VQ-2eL2XgB&index=2.

54 Kevin Goldsmith, "Thoughts on emulating Spotify's matrix organization in other companies," *Puppies, Flowers, Rainbows and Kittens*, Kevin Goldsmith, March 14, 2014, http://blog.kevingoldsmith.com/2014/03/14/thoughts-on-emulating-spotifys-matrix-organization-in-other-companies/

55 Henrik Kniberg, "Scaling Agile @ Spotify with Tribes, Squads, Chapters & Guilds," *Crisp's Blog*, Crisp AB, November 14, 2012, http://blog.crisp.se/2012/11/14/henrikkniberg/scaling-agile-at-spotify.

56 Noam Bardin, "What is a Startup CEO's real job?," LinkedIn, LinkedIn Corporation, January 3, 2015, https://www.linkedin.com/pulse/what-early-stage-startup-ceos-real-job-noam-bardin/

57 Ibid.

58 Cindy Robbins, "How Salesforce Uses Technology to Drive Alignment and Transparency," Salesforce Blog, Salesforce.com, Inc., April 2, 2018, https://www.salesforce.com/blog/2018/04/salesforce-technology-alignment-transparency.html.

59 Marc Benioff, "Marc Benioff: How to Create Alignment Within Your Company in Order to Succeed," Salesforce Blog, Salesforce.com, Inc., April 9, 2013, https://www.salesforce.com/blog/2013/04/how-to-create-alignment-within-your-company.html.

60 One of the best sources available for free to understand more about this role is the video created by Henrik Kniberg on YouTube: https://www.youtube.com/watch?v=502ILHjX9EE.

61 "Culture of Empathy Builder: Thich Nhat Hanh," Center for Building a Culture of Empathy, Edwin Rutsch, http://cultureofempathy.com/References/Experts/Thich-Nhat-Hanh.htm.

Bibliography

Apple Inc. "Apple Developer Program." Apple Developer. https://developer.apple.com/programs/.

AZQuotes.com. "Joichi Ito quote." AZ Quotes. http://www.azquotes.com/quote/731979.

Bardin, Noam. "What is a Startup CEO's real job?" LinkedIn. LinkedIn Corporation. January 3, 2015. https://www.linkedin.com/pulse/what-early-stage-startup-ceos-real-job-noam-bardin/

Bariso, Justin. "Elon Musk Takes Customer Complaint on Twitter From Idea to Execution in 6 Days." *Inc.* Manuseto Ventures. https://www.inc.com/justin-bariso/elon-musk-takes-customer-complaint-on-twitter-from-idea-to-execution-in-6-days.html.

Benioff, Marc. "Marc Benioff: How to Create Alignment Within Your Company in Order to Succeed." Salesforce Blog. Salesforce.com, Inc. April 9, 2013. https://www.salesforce.com/blog/2013/04/how-to-create-alignment-within-your-company.html.

Condé Nast. "Google X Head On Moonshots: 10x Is Easier Than 10 Percent." *Wired.* February 11, 2013, 06:30 a.m. https://www.wired.com/2013/02/moonshots-matter-heres-how-to-make-them-happen/.

Daimler. "The Mercedes-Benz F 015 Luxury in Motion." Mercedes-Benz. https://www.mercedes-benz.com/en/mercedes-benz/innovation/research-vehicle-f-015-luxury-in-motion/.

Disney. "Walt Disney's Carousel of Progress." Walt Disney World Resort (website). https://disneyworld.disney.go.com/attractions/magic-kingdom/walt-disney-carousel-of-progress/.

Edwin Rutsch. "Culture of Empathy Builder: Thich Nhat Hanh." Center for Building a Culture of Empathy. http://cultureofempathy.com/References/Experts/Thich-Nhat-Hanh.htm.

Fast Company & Inc. "Slack's Founder On How They Became a $1 Billion Company In Two Years." Fast Company. February 4, 2015. https://www.fastcompany.com/3041905/slacks-founder-on-how-they-became-a-1-billion-company-in-two-years.

Fein, Donna. "The Weirdest Interview Advice You'll Ever Get: Don't Ask Questions." CBS News. CBS Interactive Inc. Last updated November 9, 2010, 5:04 p.m. https://www.cbsnews.com/news/the-weirdest-interview-advice-youll-ever-get-dont-ask-questions/.

First Round. "From 0 to $1B - Slack's Founder Shares Their Epic Launch Strategy." First Round Review. http://firstround.com/review/From-0-to-1B-Slacks-Founder-Shares-Their-Epic-Launch-Strategy/.

First Round. "How Design Thinking Transformed Airbnb from a Failing Startup to a Billion Dollar Business." First Round Review. http://firstround.com/review/How-design-thinking-transformed-Airbnb-from-failing-startup-to-billion-dollar-business/.

Goldsmith, Kevin. "Thoughts on emulating Spotify's matrix organization in other companies." *Puppies, Flowers, Rainbows and Kittens*. Kevin Goldsmith. March 14, 2014. http://blog.kevingoldsmith.com/2014/03/14/thoughts-on-emulating-spotifys-matrix-organization-in-other-companies/

Goodreads Inc. "Quote by Helen Keller." Goodreads. https://www.goodreads.com/quotes/9411-alone-we-can-do-so-little-together-we-can-do.

GoPro, Inc. "About Us." GoPro. https://gopro.com/about-us.

Griffin, Tren. "12 Things about Product-Market Fit." *Andreessen Horowitz*. Andreessen Horowitz. February 18, 2017. http://a16z.com/2017/02/18/12-things-about-product-market-fit/.

Griffith, Erin. "Jack Dorsey's Vision for Twitter Becomes Clear." *Fortune*. Time Inc. February 11, 2016. http://fortune.com/2016/02/10/jack-dorseys-vision-for-twitter-becomes-clear/

Hadfield, Chris. "Chris Hadfield: Earth-bound." Macleans.ca. Rogers Media. October 23, 2013. http://www.macleans.ca/culture/earth-bound/.

Harpo, Inc. "Oprah Talks to Thich Nhat Hanh." Oprah.com. http://www.oprah.com/spirit/oprah-talks-to-thich-nhat-hanh.

Hartmans, Avery. "How the career of Ryan Graves, Uber's first billionaire CEO, was launched by a single tweet." *Business Insider*. Insider Inc. August 10, 2017, 2:59 p.m. http://www.businessinsider.com/ryan-graves-uber-tweet-career-2017-8.

Hollister, Sean. "Sorry, Snapchat: The glassholes are coming." CNET. CBS Interactive Inc. November 19, 2016, 5:00 a.m. https://www.cnet.com/news/snapchat-spectacles-glassholes-google-glass/.

Kniberg, Henrik. "Scaling Agile @ Spotify with Tribes, Squads, Chapters & Guilds." *Crisp's Blog.* Crisp AB. November 14, 2012. http://blog.crisp.se/2012/11/14/henrikkniberg/scaling-agile-at-spotify.

Lawton, Christopher. "Inside SAP's Skunkworks as It Takes Aim at Oracle." *The Wall Street Journal.* Dow Jones & Company Inc. January 26, 2012. https://www.wsj.com/articles/SB10001424052970203430 404577092651330963684.

Lipman, Victor. "Phil Jackson Brings NY Knicks 'Mindful' Management." *Forbes.* Forbes Media LLC. October 15, 2014, 01:01 p.m. https://www.forbes.com/sites/victorlipman/2014/10/15/phil-jackson-brings-ny-knicks-mindful-management/.

Liu, Sharky. "What is Dropbox? Explained! Original Dropbox Video [HD]." YouTube video, 2:17. June 14, 2012. https://www.youtube.com/watch?v=xy9nSnalvPc.

Makhija, Pushpa. "How to Use Cohort Analysis to Improve Customer Retention." CleverTap. WizRocket, Inc. March 28, 2016. https://clevertap.com/blog/how-to-use-cohort-analysis-to-improve-customer-retention/

Momoko Ito Foundation. "Home Page." Safecast. https://blog.safecast.org/.

Musk, Elon. Twitter post. December 17, 2016, 5:05 a.m. https://twitter.com/elonmusk/status/810108760010043392?lang=en.

Pruett, Chris. "LinkedIn Desktop Redesign Puts Conversations and Content at the Center." Official LinkedIn Blog. LinkedIn Corporation. January 19, 2017. https://blog.linkedin.com/2017/january/19/linkedin-desktop-redesign-puts-conversations-and-content-at-the-center.

Quittner, Jeremy. "Robin Chase: How I Survived a Huge Screw-up." *Inc.* Manuseto Ventures. February 28, 2013. http://www.inc.com/magazine/201303/how-i-got-started/robin-chase.html.

Robbins, Cindy. "How Salesforce Uses Technology to Drive Alignment and Transparency." Salesforce Blog. Salesforce.com, Inc. April 2, 2018. https://www.salesforce.com/blog/2018/04/salesforce-technology-alignment-transparency.html.

Roberts, Emily. "Introducing the Amazon Dash Button and Dash Replenishment Service." Appstore Blogs. Amazon.com, Inc. March 21, 2015. https://developer.amazon.com/blogs/appstore/post/Tx3N-3VXXO52B15I/introducing-the-amazon-dash-button-and-dash-replenishment-service.

Roettgers, Janko. "Roku Got Close to $400 Million Revenue in 2016." *Variety*. Variety Media, LLC. February 28, 2017, 6:00 a.m. http://variety.com/2017/digital/news/roku-2016-revenue-1201998433/

Ryerson, Lia. "There's a ride at Disney that will never shut down, no matter what — here's why." *Insider*. Insider Inc. February 21, 2018, 2:27 p.m. http://www.thisisinsider.com/disneys-carousel-of-progress-will-never-close-2018-2.

Sheridan, Richard. Twitter post. March 22, 2015, 6:02 a.m. https://twitter.com/menloprez/status/579629235720994816.

Smith, Dave. "Krystina, Avondale, Arizona." D23: The Official Disney Fan Club. Disney. https://d23.com/ask-dave/krystina-avondale-arizona-2/.

Solomon, Micah. "How To Think Like Apple About The Customer Service Experience." *Forbes*. Forbes Media LLC. November 21, 2013, 4:58 p.m. https://www.forbes.com/sites/micahsolomon/2014/11/21/how-apple-thinks-differently-about-the-customer-service-experience-and-how-it-can-help-you/#15d77bc627c9.

Statista Inc. "Number of monthly active Facebook users worldwide as of 1st quarter 2018 (in millions)." Statista. https://www.statista.com/statistics/264810/number-of-monthly-active-facebook-users-worldwide/.

Surowiecki, James. "Where Nokia Went Wrong." *The New Yorker*. Condé Nast. Updated September 3, 2013. http://www.newyorker.com/business/currency/where-nokia-went-wrong.

The Board of Regents of the University of Wisconsin. "Quotes in Statistics & Science." Department of Statistics. https://www.stat.wisc.edu/quotes.

The LEGO Group. "Successful LEGO Strategy Delivers Continued Strong Growth." About Us LEGO.com. February 21, 2013. https://www.lego.com/en-us/aboutus/news-room/2013/february/annual-result-2012.

Thomas, Owen. "Apple: Hello, iPhone." CNN Money. Cable News Network. January 9, 2007, 5:36 p.m. http://money.cnn.com/2007/01/09/technology/apple_jobs/.

Undercoffler, David. "CES 2015: Mercedes-Benz shows off self-driving car of the future." *Los Angeles Times*. Los Angeles Times. January 5, 2015, 10:58 p.m. http://www.latimes.com/business/autos/la-fi-hy-ces-2015-mercedes-autonomous-20150105-story.html.

Wikimedia Foundation. "Taxicabs of the United States." Wikipedia. Last modified June 14, 2018, 08:34. https://en.wikipedia.org/wiki/Taxicabs_of_the_United_States.

Wikimedia Foundation. "Walt Disney's Carousel of Progress." Wikipedia. Last modified May 7, 2018, 14:15. https://en.wikipedia.org/wiki/Walt_Disney%27s_Carousel_of_Progress.

About the Authors

Navjot Singh is a senior product development executive with over seventeen years in product development and product management. He has worked for many large corporations and has been responsible for the launch of many products right from their ideation toward a steady growth strategy. He has also gone through many leadership and product development programs at top tier universities like University of California at Berkeley and IIM-Ahmedabad. Nav is also an MBA from Hult International Business school in San Francisco and currently working on a startup idea and as Director for Product Management in the telecommunication industry.

Kamal Manglani coaches product executives, product management teams, and agile development organizations in large enterprises and startups. An innovator at heart, he is a seasoned executive focused on uncovering new and sometimes unconventional paths to growth. Kamal has over seventeen years of corporate, consulting, and entrepreneurial experience all geared at one thing: turning untapped potential into real customer value.

Kamal Manglani has defined new areas of agility using first principles approach, design thinking, lean startup, and Day 1 execution discipline.